W9-BLF-771

J

F

Living
With Your
Teenager

Living
With Your
Teenager

MARLENE BRUSKO

McGraw-Hill Book Company

New York   St. Louis   San Francisco   Bogotá
Guatemala   Hamburg   Lisbon   Madrid   Mexico
Montreal   Panama   Paris   San Juan
São Paulo   Tokyo   Toronto

123456789 DOCDOC 876

ISBN 0-07-008594-3

LIBRARY OF CONGRESS CATALOGING IN PUBLICATION DATA

Brusko, Marlene.
  Living with your teenager.
   1. Parenting.   2. Adolescent psychology.   3. Con-
flict of generations.   4. Youth—Education.   I. Title.
HQ755.8.B78 1986   649'.125   84-26175
ISBN 0-07-008594-3

Book design by Kathryn Parise

To

Julienne and Edward Guimond
and Eugene Bouchard

Preface

The purpose of this book is to help parents of teenagers deal with a wide variety of issues. It is direct—perhaps a little too direct if you are hurting. It provides a great deal of information, some of which may be difficult to accept when you are angry. The book is based on the firm belief that no matter how bad things are, you can do something to improve the situation. But you may not want to hear this if you are tired and feel like quitting.

If you can overcome these natural reactions and are genuinely motivated to improve your relationship with your teenager, then the ideas in this book will be helpful. None of them is a magic wand, but they all work! These suggestions should help reduce some of the negative feelings that often accompany parenting.

In addition to providing information, this book helps you distinguish between big problems and little ones. In the heat of day-to-day disagreements and frictions, it is frequently difficult to distinguish between common and harmless behavior and unusual and dangerous behavior. This book gives you guidelines, suggestions, and step-by-step procedures for solving common problems. These are based both on solid adolescent psychology and on twenty years of experience working with adolescents and their families. They have worked time and time again for other parents.

The book also gives detailed instructions for finding outside help if you have a serious problem that self-help won't solve.

This is the type of book that you can read in parts if you prefer. You can read some of it now, put it on the shelf, and take it down later to read other parts. It is designed to answer the questions that parents of teenagers ask about practically every subject related to their adolescents.

The people I have worked with over the years—high school students and their parents and teachers—are the wonderful individuals who are ultimately responsible for this book. They paid me the supreme compliment of telling me who they were—of telling me about their joy and their pain, their failures and their successes. To all of you whom I have had the pleasure of knowing—thank you! To protect your anonymity, the people in the examples are composites, and the names have been chosen at random.

I would like to express special gratitude to my husband Ralph for his help and constant support and to our three children—John, Joe, and Annie—for their patience with my imperfect parenting.

Many people were very helpful with the actual writing process also. Wendy Stebbins encouraged me to write the book. Joan Stroner provided critical assistance with her incisive editing skills. And then there were all the readers who provided commentary and suggestions: Lorna and Arnold Guimond, Marveen Forgus, Sharon Jackson, Dr. James Conroy, John Hicks, Dr. Janet Reed, and Mary Summers. To all of you, my sincere thanks.

Contents

SECTION II
Building Communication
119

SECTION I

Problems, Ideas and Solutions

Chapter 1

Aggravations

Most parents do not have serious problems with their teenagers. They have good kids and readily admit this. But it seems that one aggravation or another is always disrupting familial tranquility. Sometimes these aggravations can create so much anger that parents and teenagers unwittingly escalate a minor problem into a much bigger one.

"It's my house and my kid. As long as he's living here, he'll do it my way." There is truth in this statement, but such an attitude encourages fights instead of cooperation. Teenagers just won't be treated like chattels or little children, so the "do it or else" approach is doomed to failure. The issues are not necessarily earth-shattering either, but parents continue to nag or explode while becoming less and less effective.

This chapter is about these irritating, but not necessarily serious, areas of conflict.

CLOTHES

There are different "uniforms" for different social groups. These vary according to the community and the times, but every parent should remember this:

What parents object to may immediately become desirable.

Insisting on a bizarre wardrobe is one of the least harmful ways in which teenagers separate from parents. Why get an ulcer over it? Unreasonable parental demands in unimportant areas almost always lead to more serious problems. It just isn't worth the risk.

But if there are times when you just can't take it anymore or if clothing seems to be of real importance, try discussion. For example:

Father: Mary, it bugs the hell out of me when you wear provocative clothes and a lot of makeup, but it was very cruel of me to call you a streetwalker, and I apologize for that.

Mary: What does "provocative" mean?

Father: Overly sexy. It looks as if you're trying to turn on every guy on the street.

Mary: Is that what you think?

Father: Well, I hope it's not true. Your mother says that you're just trying to look nice and that it will take some time before you decide what styles are best for you. But when I see you in tight sweaters, no bra, and jeans you can't even sit down in, I see red. To me it looks bad, but I am willing to really try hard to ignore what you wear so that we won't have to fight so much. I hate it when we yell at each other all the time. It hurts too much.

(Notice that since this is the father's problem and not the mother's, it is the father who should discuss it. Parents won't always agree, and they should not feel obliged to gang up on their kids.)

Mary: You hurt me a lot. I don't really want to hurt you, but maybe I do. When you make me really mad and put me down, I dig around to find even tighter jeans. Sometimes I get so angry that I don't know how else to fight back.

Father: Is there a way we can work this out so that we won't get so angry?

Mary: Well, I really want to wear a bra. I just go without one to make you mad. So how about if I wear a bra and you don't call me a streetwalker?

Father: That sounds fair. Could we also agree to talk to each other each week like this—not about clothes so much—just a time when we can talk without yelling? It would help me stop yelling, I think.

Mary: OK. That sounds great.

The problem is more serious if your son or daughter is wearing the clothes that are associated with a gang or other undesirable group. In some communities, these teenagers may be on the fringe of the law or in trouble with the police.

As with any stereotype, however, it is very dangerous to assume that clothes alone are an indication of problem behavior. If there are no signs of illegal activity other than choice of clothes, don't assume the worst without checking further.

Parents have other problems with the issue of clothes. Some find it difficult to understand how important it is for adolescents to wear what everyone else is wearing. Others spend a fortune keeping their teenagers in the latest fashions. You don't want to embarrass your kids, but you also have no obligation to buy them every new fad that comes along. Staying on a middle ground is important.

One such middle-ground strategy is simply to talk about what amount of clothing money is reasonable and how it will be disbursed (for example, in monthly installments). This means preparing a careful budget, which serves two purposes: (1) It helps parents decide what is a fair amount, and (2) it helps the teenager tentatively plan expenditures. For instance, is a new coat necessary? How much might it cost? How many shirts and jeans does the teenager need?

It is important to remember, however, that the primary purpose of a budget is to establish a fair allotment. Once that amount has been determined, the teenager decides how to use it. Perhaps your daughter would rather forgo the designer jeans you budgeted for and buy an especially nice blouse instead. Possibly your son managed to find a winter coat on sale, which allowed him to buy the latest fad. The point is that once a reasonable amount has been decided on, the young adult has to make choices about how it is spent.

It is best to let the teenager make as many decisions as possible. The parents decide how much of their money will be spent, but the teenager decides what clothes to buy.

Teenagers will make mistakes. They may purchase ridiculous things and pay more than they should. Remember that this is a learning process, so a lot of inappropriate things will happen. Adolescents learn by making mistakes, as adults do. Poor decisions have their natural consequences. For example, your teenage daughter may run out of money and not be able to buy the nice sweater she wanted. This is a part of learning, and this is why it is important to agree from the beginning that anything above and beyond the amount determined has to come out of the teenager's earnings.

You will be teaching responsibility and money management, and you will be showing the respect that adolescents crave. There are some predictable pitfalls to avoid, however:

Never say "I told you so."   Bite your tongue, talk to the dog, or run around the block—do anything to avoid showing this delicious feeling of having been right.

Try hard.   Don't go through the roof when a mistake is made.

Understand.   Realize that your teenager's choices will be different from yours.

Be consistent.   Do not increase the allowance or allotment if the money runs out.

HAIR LENGTH OR STYLE

Hair length or style is a minor problem. How lucky for you if your teenager expresses that need to be different by wearing a hairstyle you don't like rather than by adopting values that go against the ones you cherish.

Teenagers need to be different from their parents.

DIRTY ROOM; MESSY HOUSE

There is only one really effective way to handle a dirty bedroom: *Close the Door.* Arguments about dirty rooms start when a child is young and frequently continue without relief until he or she moves out. They just aren't worth the pain and agony. A dirty room does not mean that your adolescent likes to live in a pigsty. Teenagers just need to feel that they control their own lives. Frequently when parents stop using a messy bedroom to badger their kids, the adolescents begin cleaning on their own. If they do—fine. But if they don't, the world will not come to an end.

Adolescents are also more likely to clean their rooms if they are able to decorate them in a way that pleases them. A new coat of paint or a new comforter can go a long way toward personalizing a room and encouraging cleanliness. However, do not bargain with your child. Don't say "I'll buy you a new lamp if you promise to keep your room clean." That will not work. In fact, it can make the situation worse. A helpful conversation might go as follows:

Mother: I've tried closing the door to your bedroom, and that helps, but I guess I would still prefer you to clean your room on a more regular basis. Am I being unreasonable?

Ellen: No. I like to see my room clean too, but sometimes I don't have the time.

Mother: Do you feel that's the biggest problem?

Ellen: Well, not really. Even though it is my room, I don't like it very much. It looks like a little kid's room or something.

Mother: How would you like to change it?

Ellen: Well, I've had that dresser since I was 2, and I'm really sick of looking at that putrid wallpaper.

Mother: Tell me about your perfect room.

Ellen: (very animated now): Well, first I would paint the walls. . . .

The perfect room would cost about $400, so Ellen and her mother devise a shared-expense, one-year plan. Now it will really be Ellen's room, and the chances of cooperation are increased. Each has had an opportunity to listen to the other.

Another very simple (not easy, just simple) way to increase cleanliness is to comment on every positive thing you can:

"Your room looks so nice when the drawers are closed" (said only when the drawers are actually closed).

"Your room looks so cheery when the spread is on."

"I really like the way you rearranged your shelves."

You will notice that these are not effusive statements, praise that isn't deserved, or veiled put-downs. They are genuine comments on specific things. They also do not make a judgment about the person. Statements like "You're such a good girl to clean your room" are almost as damaging as "You're just a dirty slob." Your teenager's worth is not based on the cleanliness of his or her room.

A more interesting problem can arise when two children share a room. Unless you are blessed with unusual progeny, one will be very neat, and the other will be a slob. The neat one then tries to draw the parents into the fight by complaining about the mold and other unusual living things left by the slob.

Parents who get involved in such fights are really asking for trouble. The two can work it out between themselves. You should refuse to get involved or to feel guilty or sorry. Consistently and firmly encourage them to work out their own problems. The parent who sides with one against the other is getting into a ridiculous and occasionally dangerous position. You should say, for example:

"I will not referee your fights. Both of you can talk this out and come up with a compromise. It is totally up to you. I will not get involved." It is possible that you will have to say this a dozen or more times, but eventually it should sink in.

Every parent in the world has tried nagging, threats, and bribes. None of these works. It is much easier to relax and try something that does work.

Of course, it almost goes without saying that by the age of 13, children should be doing most of their own cleaning. Their mothers should rarely pick up, vacuum, make the bed, or do anything else in the room. A teenager must be responsible for at least that much space in the house.

If a teenager leaves the rest of the house in a mess, that's a different matter. Common areas need common upkeep. However, merely laying down the law is not effective. Cooperation is ideal. What are some realistic ways of eliciting cooperation?

Rudolph Dreikurs, in *How to Stop Fighting with Your Kids,* firmly advocates the family council. You might want to try a modified version.

Sit down and discuss the problems of a messy house as well as the problems of cleaning. See whether you can work out a schedule of who does what and when. Be sure that everyone gets a chance to choose what he or she wants to do. These are not assigned tasks. Make a list, or, better still, let one of the kids make a list. This list, of course, includes what Mom and Dad are going to do toward the common good. If Mom washes the clothes and cooks dinner, this should be listed. All household chores and who is responsible for them are listed.

Not one word is uttered all week about chores. If the children are not overly cooperative, many of the chores will not be done by the end of the week. Have another meeting and ask everyone how this situation should be handled. Define the problem: Everyone agreed to do certain things, but some members of the family blew it. Ask for suggestions about what should happen if chores are not completed. For example:

Father: Well, how did we do with the chores this week?

Allen: Sarah didn't wash the dishes Friday, so I didn't
(age 13) have a cereal bowl Saturday morning.

Sarah: You little brat. You didn't clean under the chairs
(age 15) in the TV room.

Mother: May I make a suggestion? Let's all agree that no one of us will blame anyone else. We are responsible for what we have agreed to do, and it is also our responsibility to evaluate our own performance. I, for instance, agreed to clean the bathroom, but I was so busy this week that I didn't do a very good job of it. I think I did everything else on my list, though.

Allen: Well, I forgot to take the garbage out a couple of times, and it did smell.

Father: What can we do about that?

Allen: Maybe you could remind me.

Father: No, Allen. I'm sure you can devise a way to remind yourself. Otherwise, it will be back to the way it was.

Allen: Oh, all right. I suppose I could leave a note on my alarm clock.

Mother: That's a good idea. Do whatever helps you remember on your own.

It is very important that chores left undone not be done by someone else. It would be much easier to take the garbage out yourself, but then nothing changes. Be patient! Try it again for another week. Be generous with your compliments when improvements occur.

The following are some essential elements of this plan of action.

Persistence

The plan won't work after a week. Or, what is more common, it will work for two weeks, and then the children will stop doing their chores. Hang in there! Keep meeting for a short period each week or perhaps twice a week. Change responsibilities as frequently as your family desires. Don't let this be a flash in the pan, with Mom and Dad nagging but doing everything again. There will be an overwhelming temptation to scrap the whole thing as useless and revert to the screaming, pleading, threatening ways of before. These ways may not work well, but they are familiar.

The big question is: "Do you really want your children to help enough so that you are willing to stick to a difficult but workable approach?" It is quite possible that your answer is "no." But if it is, realize that you are making a choice. You are not a victim. You are cooperating in maintaining the status quo.

Hope

Believe in yourself and in your children. When kids are given genuine responsibilities, they usually come through very well indeed. Once the power struggle has ended ("You *will* do this"—"You can't make me"), real cooperation ensues. You will never have perfection, but as long as you can accept that, the situation should improve a great deal.

BLARING MUSIC

Loud music can be allowed within moderation. However, no one should cause another family member undue discomfort with loud music or anything else, for that matter.

In a home where there is cooperation, teenagers usually play their music loud, but within reasonable limits. Compromise is the best policy. Yelling to "shut that damn thing off" may be exercising parental authority, but negotiating the level of noise is more productive. Since most stereos have numbers or other markings on the volume control, compromise about where the control should be set when parents are present is helpful. If the music continues to blare, ask whether it can be turned down to the agreed-upon volume. If that doesn't work, then loud music is not the issue. Perhaps you are in an ongoing power struggle. Your teenager is trying to get even. Blaring music is merely a symptom of a much larger problem.

PHONE USE

Humorists who write about adolescents have a great time with the phone. Joke upon joke is made about overuse. Even the phone company capitalized on this a few years ago with a commercial for phone service stores. The new phone is plugged in, and within seconds a call comes through for one of the teenagers. The implication—which is often the reality—is that the call goes on forever.

All right, everyone knows that parents of teenagers have this problem. It isn't an embarrassing problem, not one that you try to hide. But even though it is common, it is very, very irritating. The jokes may be funny, but trying to call home for an hour when the car has broken down definitely is not. Neither is missing an important business call or having the blasted thing ring from morning until night. But, as is true of so many other things we have discussed, if this is your biggest problem, you are fortunate indeed. However, when counting your blessings wears a little thin, what else can be done about phone use?

Some families try to solve the problem by getting the adolescent his or her own phone. This is not normally recommended. If the adolescent pays for the phone, it is a little better, but it is still an expensive alternative. Use of the phone provides excellent lessons in cooperation, *but* constant fighting about phone use is rarely productive. Make the decision on the basis of your circumstances and resources.

Other families have resorted to a "call waiting" feature. When the phone is in use and another call is made to your number, a clicking noise notifies you that someone else is calling. This can prevent you from missing important calls and can reduce some of the other friction related to phone use. It is also a nuisance, and although it is not as expensive as a second line, it does cost money. But if it ends fighting and missing important calls, it is probably worth it.

Other approaches involve cooperation. Some families find that a time limit on calls works—sometimes. Time limits, however, need to apply to all members of the family, not just the children. Therefore, it seems unrealistic to set five or ten minutes as a limit. It should also be possible to make longer calls at times when other calls are not as likely. Teenagers can be asked not to use the phone when business calls are expected. A family that has learned to cooperate can work around this problem quite well.

Time need not be measured with a stopwatch, either. When Jane's friend has a terrible problem that she needs to talk about, it would be appropriate for Jane to ask the other family members whether she can stay on the phone a little longer. The point is that all family members should respect the rights of others in the family when it comes to using the phone as well as in other areas.

GETTING UP IN THE MORNING

Children past the age of 6 or 7 usually should not have to be awakened by a parent.

Parents should not have to awaken teenagers.

Each child should have his or her own alarm clock. Getting out of bed is the child's responsibility, not the parent's.

So the first step in putting the responsibility where it belongs is to buy an alarm clock. With a cooperative but sleepy teenager, an alarm and a pleasant discussion may be all you need. If you have already tried that without success, it may be necessary to go a step further. If your child already has an alarm clock but doesn't hear it, he or she chooses not to hear it to keep you involved. After making sure that there are no physical reasons for not hearing the alarm, explain what you will do:

> "Beginning tomorrow morning, I will not wake you up. You have an alarm clock, and it is your responsibility to get out of bed. If you are late for school, I will call and say you overslept, but I will not make excuses for you. You will have to deal with the school about whatever consequences follow.

I also will not drive you to school if you miss the bus. I am tired of fighting with you about this. I don't want to make you into a little kid by assuming responsibility that is yours."

Then *stick to it!* That is the hardest and most important aspect of all. It is almost guaranteed that your child will over-sleep many times. He or she must handle the consequences of this behavior. You must not wake your teenager up or bail him or her out by making excuses or providing a ride to school.

Remember that getting out of bed is a decision, albeit a difficult one for some. What are the chances that your son will get up on his own to go to a ball game with a friend? What are the chances that your daughter will get up on her own on a day when she is planning to drive to the next town to attend a concert?

If you have followed through and your teenager still isn't getting up consistently after one or two months, you have a bigger problem. Getting up in the morning is one of your less serious concerns.

FIGHTING SIBLINGS

"I'm so sick of the fighting between my kids that I could just scream. When will they ever stop this?" Fortunately, there are effective means of dealing with this problem. Adolescence is a little late to begin, but all is not lost.

Fighting has a purpose. It rarely occurs simply because children don't like each other or because they just can't get along. Children begin fighting in the early years to get the parents' attention or to drive them crazy. There is real power in the ability to pull Mother away from whatever she is doing to come and break up a fight. It also helps children establish their roles in the family. One becomes the good, abused kid, while another is the bad, mean kid. Children need a place and would much rather receive attention for being "bad" than no atten-tion at all or less than what they feel they need.

Jim is a 14-year-old who appears very immature because he continually picks on Sarah, who is 11. What their parents don't realize is that Sarah is cooperating in all this and is as much to blame as Jim.

Jim is quietly watching TV. Sarah comes into the room and sits near him. She "accidentally" kicks him while trying to get comfortable. Jim says, "Leave me alone!" because he knows it wasn't accidental. Sarah says, "Baby!" and Jim swats her. She now kicks him hard, and he shoves her off the couch. Sarah runs to her mother and complains about her mean brother. Their mother comes into the TV room, looks at Jim sternly, and says, "When are you ever going to grow up? Pick on someone your own size for a change."

Jim protests with, "She kicked me first."

"But he pushed me off the couch," responds the abused 11-year-old.

Their mother then says, "Just shut up, or I'm going to send both of you to your rooms."

"Why should I go to my room when it's his fault?" whines Sarah.

This can go on for some time, as everyone who is familiar with the process knows. The alternative is for their mother to *stay out of the fight!* She should not take sides or even discuss the matter. When Sarah comes running to her, she should say, "I'm sure you can handle this yourself."

Assigning blame never solves the problem.

Difficult? Of course it's difficult, especially if the fighting has been going on for ten or more years. But refusing to take sides is the only way to maintain your sanity and hope to stop the fighting. Be honest, now; you have tried everything else, and it hasn't worked. Why continue self-defeating behavior?

The first step is not to run to the scene of the crime. If you remain absent, it is almost guaranteed that the martyr in your family will come to enlist your aid. Now you must act very unconcerned and simply assure your child that he or she can handle the situation. Do not become involved; do not take sides; do not make any judgment whatsoever.

If and when you begin acting this way, it will truly confuse your kids. They won't believe you are for real. So they may up the ante. That is, they may scream louder, get bloody instead of just bruised, etc. No one will really get hurt except by choice. *No one is being abused!* All the kids cooperate in the fight. The "good" kid needs to be knocked around to get your sympathy and protection, and the "bad" kid needs to have you yell so that he or she will still get your attention. Neither position is any good. The situation needs to be stopped.

It is possible that initially you will not be able to stand the fighting without making a response. If so, leave. Go to the bathroom and run the water to shut out the noise, go to your bedroom and play the radio very loud, or even leave the house if necessary. Do whatever you have to do to stay out of it.

It is also important to speak as little as possible. After saying, "I'm sure you can handle this yourself," be prepared for tears and a great deal of pressure: "But, Mom, he hurt me bad; look, I'm bleeding." The wailing will get louder, and the pained look on the child's face will be heartrending. Do not say another word. If you want to, repeat what you said and then walk away.

If you maintain this "stay out of it" behavior consistently during the grade school years, the fighting will be reduced fairly quickly. By the time your children have reached adolescence, it may take much longer, and perhaps the fighting will never stop enough to please you. However, you no longer need to become involved or get angry. It is their problem; no one is more at fault than anyone else—no matter how it looks.

There is another reason why parents may find this approach very difficult. As children grow older, many parents find it nearly impossible to accept the fact that soon their help will no longer be needed. The empty-nest syndrome is real, and for some parents it is extremely painful. Staying involved as much as possible—even in their children's fights—is a small way in which parents can still feel needed and useful. This isn't good for the parents, and it is worse for the children. It is a common reaction and is nothing to be ashamed of, but it is healthy to realize what you are doing and to stop it.

This discussion, of course, has to do with normal kids and normal fighting. If one of your children actually abuses you or one of the children, that is a serious situation that needs immediate therapeutic intervention. There are no quick answers for real abuse. Such situations include deliberate beatings, abnormal cruelty (killing someone's pet, starting vicious rumors, etc.), rape, serious blackmail. These and similar situations are way beyond self-help.

"YOU NEVER TALK TO ME ANYMORE."

This is usually a mother's message to a daughter who is growing up normally, although fathers often feel the same. The daughter shares secrets with her friends, asks their advice, and cries on their shoulders, and she really wants fewer "good talks" with her mother.

It is also possible that the son or daughter begins confiding in another adult, such as a teacher or counselor at school, a neighbor, or Aunt Sally—just about anyone but the mother or father. Parents begin feeling very rejected and believe that their relationship with their children is deteriorating. Their son or daughter used to tell them everything, and now it's a big day if they find out who their teenager is going to the dance with.

Hang in there, parents. It hurts, but it is part of a necessary process. Remember that your children love you, even if they don't talk to you as much as they used to. It does not mean that they see you as untrustworthy. It just means that they are growing up.

One 16-year-old girl explains her side of the situation as follows:

> "I get home from school; I'm tired, and I just want to listen to the stereo for a few minutes. But my mom wants to sit and talk about my day. If I say everything was fine, she pouts the rest of the evening. She wants to hear about my

thoughts and gut-level feelings. And I just don't want to talk to her about that all the time. I feel as if I can't breathe when she's around—as if she's an albatross around my neck. I really wish she would yell. I could deal with that. I just don't know how to get her to stop smothering me."

This girl is trying to separate, and her mother refuses to let go.

Her mother explains it this way:

"My daughter and I have always been very close. She tells me everything—or at least she did. I felt so close to her when I could hold her and we just cried together. I hear so much about the difficulties of adolescence. I want to be supportive and provide her the protection and help she needs. So many parents don't appreciate their kids or even help them. I always want to be there for my daughter."

This is a wonderful, warm, caring person. She is so wonderful who would want to leave her? That is the problem. Her daughter knows she has to pull away, but it will be difficult to do because the relationship is so comforting. This mother needs to realize that separation is imperative to her daughter's growth and that she must help with the process. Painful? Yes. Necessary? Absolutely! Once the daughter has separated, the chances are that their relationship will be very close again. And it will be close by mutual choice.

"THEY NEVER WANT TO DO ANYTHING WITH US ANYMORE."

Good! If your teenager would rather spend Sunday afternoon with friends than go to a movie with you, don't feel rejected. Be thrilled and relieved that he or she is growing up.

This is not easy for many parents to take, but the fact is that children will spend less time with their parents as they grow older.

"Quality" time with parents is as important in adolescence as it was in childhood. But now the emphasis is certainly more on quality than on quantity. It may be difficult to find times when you can be with your teenagers. But don't give up. Don't smother them, but don't ignore them either.

A younger teenager can be especially exasperating. Your daughter may be out or locked in her room six nights a week while you sit home. You go out on the seventh night and are greeted upon your return with, "Gee, you're never home anymore." You feel yourself torn between anger and guilt. Forget both; they waste too much energy. It's simpler to say, "Sometimes I miss you too."

An older adolescent can present other challenges. What happens when the entire family is invited to Grandma's house and Jim (age 17) has made other plans? Explain to Jim that Grandma will miss him. Then say, "What do you think you could do so that she won't feel too bad?"

Jim: I suppose I could call her and talk awhile. I think she'll understand.

Father: She probably will. Calling her sounds like a good idea.

Then when the rest of the family arrives at Grandma's house, *no one should make excuses for Jim!* It is Jim's responsibility to keep Grandma's feelings from being hurt, not yours. He is not there, and if that does not please Grandma, it is Jim's problem. She may try to make it your problem. Refuse to accept this: "Mom, I think you'd better talk to Jim about it."

Another common avoidance tactic is the "stay in the bedroom till I rot" syndrome. The teenager comes into the house, mumbles at best, makes a mad dash for his or her bedroom, and appears only to eat, use the phone, or do something else essential.

Sometimes teenagers do this to protect themselves from fighting, insults, and generally unpleasant circumstances in the home. Disturbed adolescents may use their rooms to hide from the world. However, in most cases room-bound teenagers are there because they want to be. They are there because they don't get a big kick out of watching TV with Mom and Dad anymore. It is the next best thing to getting an apartment. Why this should anger or hurt parents is not clear to adolescents. It is very difficult for most parents to let go—to allow their teenagers to grow up, move out, and be on their own. As a result, parents may feel that their children are rejecting them, when in fact they are merely growing up. It is all right for most teenagers to spend time in their rooms; it is all right for them to speak less and less to their parents. They need to separate, and initially they will have to go overboard to do it right.

The purpose of adolescence is to separate from parents.

_____Chapter 2_____

Headaches

TIME TO BE IN

Frequently, with really cooperative teenagers, a curfew seems silly. If they always come in at a reasonable time, why set another rule? Many teenagers like to test their limits though, so with them it is appropriate to set mutually acceptable times for coming in during the week and on weekends. Since this is so dependent on age and type of neighborhood, it is difficult to say what is right for everyone. However, 9 P.M. to 10 P.M. during the week (when there is school the next day) and 11 P.M. to 1 A.M. on weekends are usually considered reasonable. It is not reasonable to negotiate different hours for daughters and sons. Age and environmental circumstances are the determining factors, not sex.

Parents who feel their power slipping hang on to time limits with the pride of Custer at his last stand. Time is so objective and exact. It is by far the favorite weapon for keeping control. Adolescents sense this desperation and tend to push to the limit. They may even resort to parking the car somewhere and sitting there alone for an hour or more, rather than going home at a time that would please their parents.

If parents can pull out of the fight, their teenager will usually begin coming in much earlier. Agree on a time, but don't be unreasonable. If the adolescent is a little late, it is no tragedy. If he or she is late all the time, discuss what might be wrong. If the situation improves—fine. If it doesn't, ask your teenager to suggest consequences. Coming in an hour earlier for the next week is a possibility. Allow your young adult to make the suggestions, and don't enforce consequences without a warning.

Adolescents who are out of control stay out as long as they wish and go out whenever they want. Most will boldly walk out the front door, pushing parents out of their way if necessary. Others will sneak out a bedroom window. If the situation is this bad in your house, you are beyond self-help. Seek professional help immediately, either from the school or from a private source. No teenager should have this kind of power. (See Chapters 5 and 6 for more details.)

USE OF THE FAMILY CAR

"Can I have the car tonight?" The question ranges from mildly irritating to downright angering, depending on how often it is asked, how many plans you have to change, and how much responsibility your son or daughter exhibits.

Like responses to so many other situations, answers to this question run the gamut. Some parents fail to impose adequate limits, allowing their teenager to take the car too often and frequently changing their own plans to accommodate their manipulative little darling.

More common, however, are parents who never allow their adolescents to drive the family car or who give them such a hard time about it that it's hardly worth the effort to ask. No good purpose is served by refusing to allow a teenager to use the car for reasonable or necessary purposes. Using the car to go to work (if it's too far, too cold, or too dangerous to walk) and occasionally to go out with friends is reasonable. However, it is also reasonable to expect adolescents who are working to pay for their share of the costs of insurance and gasoline.

Many parents who refuse to allow their teenagers to use the car are just plain frightened:

"What if she gets in an accident?"

"I don't want him dragging with the car, the way I used to."

Fear is understandable. It's part of being a parent. Parents just have to live with their fears or overcome them. They can't stop their adolescents from growing.

CAR OWNERSHIP

Many high school students should not own their own cars, but many others can handle this large responsibility quite well. How do you decide?

- Can you and/or your teenager afford a car? Who will buy it and who will keep it running?

Your adolescent should usually do at least one or the other. This teaches important lessons in responsibility. But it can also create a problem. School officials have consistently found that many teenagers who own their own cars redirect their priorities at a very inappropriate time. Some adolescents (especially boys) will drop out of school altogether in order to work more hours to support the car. It takes a lot of money to keep a car running, even when the teenager can do most of the work on it. Insurance is also very expensive. Then there are the unofficial dropouts who take only easy courses or rearrange their schedules so that they can work thirty or forty hours a week to support a car. School becomes a nuisance. It is more important to maintain and improve the car. That brings us to the next questions that you must answer before you decide about car ownership:

- Is your adolescent responsible enough to keep car owner-ship in perspective?
- Is public transportation readily available, making car own-ership less necessary?
- Has your adolescent earned the "right" to car ownership?

Don't be unreasonable here, but remember that a car is a privilege, not a necessity. Also be aware, however, that a car should not be a bribe for better behavior: "If you promise not to stay out until 5 A.M. anymore, I'll buy you a car." Deal with misbehavior as it occurs and keep a car out of it.

If your adolescent is irresponsible beyond normal limits, that's a reason for you to deny car ownership, even if you can afford it:

Father: You have not earned the right to own a car.
Son: What's that supposed to mean?
Father: You tell me. Explain how you show responsibility on a day-to-day basis.
Son: Well, what if I start passing my courses and coming in on time?
Father: When that occurs, we can discuss this again. But be aware that I'm not making any promises. It's just that right now there is simply nothing to discuss.

"GIMME, GIMME, GIMME"

If this is a problem with your adolescent, it isn't something that just started. It began when your child first screamed or otherwise made a scene in the grocery store and, rather than suffer the embarrassment of continued misbehavior, you bought whatever the youngster wanted. If your habit of giving in has been going on since your child was little, it is likely to take some time and trauma to change the pattern; however, if you are successful, your teenager will have a much better time in adulthood.

Where do you begin? Actually, it is very simple—not easy, mind you, just simple. You don't need to become angry; actually, you are much better off not feeling anger, or at least not showing it in this circumstance. Just say "no" firmly and consistently. Consistency does not mean saying "no" to everything. It means simply that once you have said "no" to something, *don't change your mind.*

This discussion is not intended to make parents more likely to say "no" when the request is very reasonable. Here I am speaking only to those parents who say "yes" too much.

Do your children have more clothes than they need or perhaps more records, stereos, TVs, or electronic games than most other children have? Do you feel pressured by your children to buy things which you really can't afford or which you feel are inappropriate or not necessary? If so, you should practice saying "no."

It can be guaranteed that your adolescent will rebel, kick, scream, and otherwise cause you grief, but limits are necessary when it comes to material things, just as they are necessary when there is a problem with behavior. Stand firm; be consistent. If you're lucky—if your adolescent is lucky—the "gimme" behavior can be changed significantly before he or she moves out of the house. A parent can begin being firm by having a discussion like the following:

Mary: Mom, I need new shoes.

Mother: I just bought you a pair last week.

Mary: I know, but they don't match my new skirt.

Mother: I'm sorry they don't match, but I'm not buying you another pair of shoes.

Mary: Well, what am I supposed to do? Throw the skirt away?

Mother: I'm confident you can figure something out.

Mary: You have more than five pairs of shoes. You always get what you want.

Mother: I'm sorry, Mary, I am not buying any more shoes for you until September. We discussed this last week, and you agreed.

Mary: But, Mom, do you want me to look like a jerk?

Mother: (silence)

Mary: I *have to have* new shoes.

Mother: (quietly, but firmly): *No.*

Mary: You're so mean. I hate you!

This is a great start. It is possible that Mary's mother could have talked a little less, but since this is new behavior, it is just fine. It is almost guaranteed that the shoes will be brought up again, but no matter what plan Mary devises, her mother's answer should be *"No."*

There are other important lessons to learn from this dialogue:

- In an exchange like this, you need not justify your behavior. The reason for your "no" is obvious. Mary's attempt to work around the "no" is purely manipulative.

- Demands, put-downs, and hateful statements are best ignored in such a situation. They are used to manipulate. Your teenager will continue using them only if they are effective. If you do not respond, they lose their effectiveness.

- "Why?" should be answered only when your response is not clear. In a quiet, nice discussion, "why?" is a legitimate question. In an angry, "I want my way!" exchange, "why?" should never be answered.

- In an angry exchange, *never defend yourself.* For instance, when Mary accused her mother of being selfish, her mother might have said: "Oh, no I'm not; how dare you say that," or "When I was your age, I didn't get a new pair of shoes every week," or "You don't know how much I've sacrificed," or "You ungrateful brat!" Such responses keep the argument going. They make it possible to escalate an unreasonable request into a major confrontation. Mary's reasoning is simple: "If I can't have the shoes, at least I'll make her suffer." There is no need for this. Simply say *"No!"*

In this exchange, a father is standing firm:

Tom: Dad, drive me to Bob's house.
Father: Excuse me?
Tom: Drive me to Bob's house.
Father: No, Tom. You can walk or take your bike.

Tom: But you've always done it before. It'll only take a few minutes.
Father: Tom, you can walk or take your bike.
Tom: Boy, talk about selfish!

Tom leaves in a huff and rides his bike to Bob's house. After his father has responded in this way a few times, he can turn in his chauffeur's hat. Tom does not need to be driven everywhere. In fact, children should usually not be driven unless it is much too far, much too cold, or much too dangerous for them to walk or ride a bike.

The only answer to an unreasonable request is a firm "No!"

TEMPER TANTRUMS

Most adolescents will lose their temper or express their anger on occasion. This is normal and healthy. But repeated "explosions" that feel controlling or manipulative are another matter.

If your adolescent qualifies as a spoiled child, it will be as difficult for you to change *your* behavior as it will be for your teenager to change his or her behavior. Parents of such adolescents frequently cave in when the going gets rough. This makes the situation worse instead of better. In other words, unless you are ready to really follow through on your "no," your situation will be worse than it was before. Even if you do stand firm, things will certainly get worse before they get better. There are no easy, overnight solutions. Young adults who have gotten what they want for a number of years will be angry and confused when parents change their game plan.

Jim, age 14, knows that when his parents say "no," they mean "maybe." He knows that it takes constant nagging and sometimes sulking or a good temper tantrum to get the "yes" he wants. If Jim's parents start saying "no" and sticking to it, he will up the ante and try more serious expressions of disappointment, such as kicking the door, verbally attacking his parents, or throwing things around the room.

Jim's parents finally realize that they have to do something to regain some sense of sanity in the family. So when Jim asks for a motorcycle, they decide (1) that they can't afford it and (2) that Jim does not need it. They tell him "no" and also add that it won't do him any good to keep begging. They are firm in their "no."

Jim says nothing, but the next day he asks his father when they can go shopping for a motorcycle. His father explains that there will be no motorcycle. Jim goes into the pleading part of past interactions:

> *Jim:*   But, Dad, everyone else has one; I really feel like a fool being the only one who doesn't have a motorcycle. Other parents buy them for their kids. Why shouldn't you?
>
> *Father:* (silence)
>
> *Jim:*   I'll clean the basement and do other jobs around the house to earn it.
>
> *Father:* Jim, there will be no motorcycle.

Jim is now past pleading and goes into a rage. He swears, calls his parents "rotten," storms out of the house, and does not return until after dinner.

In the past such behavior made Jim's parents angry and they yelled at him, but there were no consequences. This time the food has been put away, and the table has been cleared. "Where's my dinner?" he demands. This time there is *no* yelling on the parents' part. Jim's mother tells him that he has missed dinner, period! Jim is really angry now. He fixes himself a sandwich and leaves a big mess in the kitchen. His father asks him to clean up the mess; the only response is more swearing. (Swearing should not be tolerated either, but take things one step at a time. For further discussion of this problem, see Chapter 12.) Jim is told that he will not sleep tonight until the mess is cleaned up.

Jim goes to his room. An hour later, Jim is asleep, and the kitchen is still a mess. His father wakes him up and guides him to the kitchen. Jim does clean up. Eventually consistency will win out. However, when consistency fails, that's the first sign that your teenager's behavior is out of control and that professional intervention may be needed. (See Chapters 5 and 6.)

Parents should never be bullied by temper tantrums or anything that comes close. This posture begins when the child is in the cradle. Giving in to temper tantrums and unreasonable demands is a dangerous pattern to establish. Breaking the pattern in adolescence is very difficult, but you will do your child a great service by changing your response behavior. The spoiled adult is even sadder than the spoiled child.

There is another hint that has helped parents in this situation:

Don't say "yes" or "no" right away when your teenager asks for something.

Instead, say that (1) you want to think about it (for a minute, an hour, a day, or a week) and (2) you want to discuss it with someone else (your spouse or another adult, never another child). This "time out" will help you avoid making snap decisions that you will regret later. There are many times when we say "yes" or "no" and later wish that we had made the other decision. Delaying the decision, even slightly, will help you make the right one. Then when you say "yes" or "no," it will be easier to stick to it.

PART-TIME JOBS; USE AND MISUSE OF MONEY

Part-time jobs are usually very helpful in a number of ways. The teenager has a chance to be successful in a different arena. For those who are not great students, the opportunity to feel successful at work can be very important. It is a source of pride and provides a way to feel more independent and resourceful.

Parents should monitor the number of hours worked and the time the adolescent returns home on school nights. Otherwise, a part-time job can interfere with school. But part-time jobs do not usually create this problem. The biggest problem, discussed earlier in this chapter, occurs when the teenager takes the job to pay for a car or its upkeep.

A job also provides additional money, which can be very helpful in many families, but it can also be a new source of conflict if the situation is not handled properly. Making money for the first time frequently leads to a number of excesses that confuse, worry, and occasionally anger the young person's parents.

Earnings from a part-time job are minimal in our economy, but if the parents provide the necessities, teenagers have what many parents consider a great deal of money to spend on themselves. They may begin buying records in alarming numbers and eating out frequently—much more frequently than the parents. They may purchase expensive cameras or automobile accessories, stereos, and other luxuries that begin to worry their parents. Little or no money may go into a savings account. What comes in, goes out quickly, and for frivolous purchases. Parents ask themselves:

"How will he ever learn the value of a dollar?"

"She has no idea what it costs to live; this extra money is making her believe that extravagant purchases are necessities."

"They don't realize what it costs to house, feed, and clothe a family; if they don't learn soon, they will end up in poverty."

The worries continue in this vein, but harping does not seem to help. Parents go through the "when I was your age" routine so often that teenagers cease even to listen.

There are ways to solve this problem, but there are no effective or recommended ways in which parents can force a teenager to handle money the way they would.

First of all, adolescents do not grow up perfect. No matter how trite that sounds, it is a fact that is constantly forgotten. Parents want their teenagers to benefit from the parents' mistakes. Why should the kids make the same mistakes the parents made? All you have to do is tell them the pitfalls, and they can then avoid them. Wrong! It would be nice if it worked that way, but there is no use wishing; it just does not happen. Your children need to make mistakes, they need to learn on their own, and they need to experiment, get hurt, and get rewards—to grow up. And they need to do this with support instead of scorn or hearing "I told you so."

By the time children are old enough to get a job, they are old enough to handle their own money. It is good if parents help the young person open a savings account or give the teenager full control of one that already exists, but it is usually fruitless to require that he or she put a certain percentage of the money earned in the account. Adolescents have to learn this on their own. They need this time to develop their own self-discipline. They are too old to be treated like little children. Forcing them to save will only encourage rebellion and delay the growing-up process.

If you really feel that your teenager's expenditures are way out of line, you may make some agreements about shifting financial responsibility in some areas. For instance, perhaps the new earner can begin buying his or her own clothes or saving for a college education. However, it is important to discuss this in such a way that it does not come across sounding like a punishment for spending money inappropriately. This will result in an adversary situation which will create more problems than it solves. It is much more growth-producing if the teenager sees the new responsibility as an additional opportunity for self-sufficiency.

There is a rule of thumb about adolescents' use of money that can help parents understand this problem. If you save a great deal of money, your oldest child will probably also save, but the other kids will spend money like crazy. The oldest is more frequently the "good" kid who doesn't rebel as much and who tries to do as he or she is told. The second-born son or daughter, on the other hand, may be a freer spirit. Second-borns often are friendlier, get into more trouble, and drive you nuts. The corollary, of course, is that spendthrift parents tend to have children who save their money.

It is rare for all the children in the family to exhibit the same saving and/or spending habits. The danger then is that the parents will pick out the one who is most like them and use this child as an example: "Why don't you save money the way Susie does?" Avoid making comparisons like this unless you are devoted to major hassles and total frustration.

Use of money is a very individual habit that is not easily altered by parents.

VACATIONS

Adolescents have jobs, can't leave their friends for a week, and don't really enjoy going on vacations with their parents anymore. How will they be supervised while the parents are away? They may be too old to hire someone to watch them, but the parents feel they are too young to be left alone.

Age, maturity, and level of cooperation in the home are the important things to consider. There is no one hard-and-fast rule. The only thing that comes close to a rule is that adolescents are usually ready to stay at home alone much sooner than their parents are ready to allow them to.

If you do let your teenager stay at home alone, it is best to leave all the phone numbers where you can be reached. Also arrange for relatives or neighbors to check in periodically and to be available in case of emergency. You should also sign the appropriate medical forms for any teenagers under 18 so that neighbors can get medical treatment for them if necessary without delay.

Frequently the biggest fear that parents have is that two teenagers will kill each other if they are left alone. That should not normally be your biggest worry. The chances are very good that they fight to get your attention or to drive you crazy, so when you are not there, the problem probably gets better, not worse. Your week or two away is a good time to think about how you will stay out of their fights from now on.

A second fear is that the teenager will have wild parties. If things are very shaky in your house, it is possible that something like this will happen. You can choose not to leave your adolescent alone or you can request that a neighbor or relative visit the house frequently. Many teenagers love this opportunity to prove their maturity. They don't want to mess it up by having wild parties. But when in doubt, take precautions.

A 16-year-old boy who had been in enough minor trouble to worry his parents said this:

> "I couldn't believe they left me alone. It was so great to have them trust me again. My friends called and wanted to come over for a party, but I told them 'no way.' Then just to be sure they wouldn't come over anyway, I locked up the house and went to Sylvia's for the evening. I think the next time my parents do this, I won't tell anyone they're leaving. Sure it was just a couple of days, but to me it meant the world."

DATING

Dating is a big headache for far too many parents—especially parents of girls and/or parents who "had to get married."

Girls usually begin dating somewhere between the eighth grade and their senior year in high school. Boys are one to two years behind. Dating later is not an advantage. In fact, adolescents who date little or who begin to date much later tend to get too serious too fast.

The intensity of adolescent love can frighten parents unnecessarily. In an attempt to lessen the attachment, parents will nag, plead, sermonize, threaten, belittle, and forbid. Most of these approaches will not change the relationship—except perhaps to draw the lovebirds closer together.

> *Parents cannot effectively control, regulate, or direct adolescents' attachments to other people.*

If you can accept that, it will save you a great deal of personal grief and will prevent intensification of a relationship that scares or worries you.

Nagging and sermonizing only reinforce the teenager's perception that the parents are outdated individuals. Pleading may make the adolescent feel guilty, but it won't change his or her behavior. Making threats and unreasonable rules will send the young couple underground. These methods encourage or necessitate deceit and circuitous planning, and most frequently they intensify the love. It becomes a matter of "us against the world." That can be dangerous. In fact, it can lead to an unhappy marriage.

This does not mean that your feelings need to be hidden or that your guidance is not necessary. On the contrary, this is a critical time to offer direction and support. But this is definitely not the time to say "Do it because I say so."

It is helpful to sit down with your son or daughter and explain how you feel. Don't present arguments and do use "I" statements (discussed in Chapter 9). The purpose is to tell your teenager how you feel, not what to do. For instance:

> "I know you are too old for me to tell you whom you can date and whom you can't. But I just need to tell you how I feel about you and Dan. I care a great deal about you, and it's difficult for me to see you grown up enough to date and fall in love. I like Dan [if you really do], but I'm worried that you're getting too serious. It's difficult for me just to say, 'Well, it's her life; I can't worry about it.' I'm afraid you might get hurt."

This approach opens lines of communication. It makes it safe for your teenager to talk to you. You might also simply say, "Tell me about Dan." The important thing is to keep talking without being negative. Young adults need an opportunity to talk to their parents, but they will not do so if there is a good chance of getting a negative response.

Parents who directly or indirectly push their children to date also create a problem. They are probably the same ones who will soon push their children to marry and then, three months after the wedding, ask whether a grandchild is on the way. Adolescents will date if they want to and when they want to. Prodding, making hints, and otherwise exerting pressure are put-downs that a teenager doesn't need.

Another problem comes up fairly frequently. The parents "adopt" the young person their son or daughter is dating. They aren't just friendly and happy to see that person, which is nice; they try to become his or her parents for most intents and purposes.

Some adolescents have a very bad homelife. It is sad for teenagers to have to go home each night to drunken, crazy, or abusive parents. Adolescents have to deal with many very undesirable circumstances. In some situations the homelife is basically very good, but the parents and the teenagers are in open warfare, making the home an unpleasant place to be.

If your son or daughter is dating someone with these problems, it is tempting to try to make up for the real or supposed injuries, to make up for what the youngster is missing. Your heart goes out, and you become very involved in listening, giving support, and occasionally providing shelter.

Such kindness and concern are heartwarming and teach your child an important lesson: to be kind, considerate, and helpful to others. Telling teenagers to behave this way is not enough. Actions always speak louder than words.

However, the problems involved also make this a very risky act of kindness:

- It is possible that the person your teenager is dating is precipitating many of the problems he or she describes at home. "Saving" the teenager from these problems will never help him or her face the issue and work at a solution.
- This youngster would rather be with you than with his or her parents and therefore tends to be at your house an inordinate amount of time. Both young people in this situation can become very isolated if they are always together. They may lose their other friends and become too emotionally dependent on each other.
- Your son or daughter may lose all sense of privacy and separateness; this is not a good thing in adolescence.
- What do you do when they fight or break up? It is hard to

listen and sympathize with either of them without showing favoritism. Your son or daughter may resent the absence of your support.

- The biggest problem, however, is what to do when they go their separate ways. If your teenager wants the relationship to end, he or she may feel guilty about depriving the other person of your love and support also. The person your teenager is dating may be reluctant to break off a relationship that is no longer desirable because he or she fears losing your support.

There are no easy solutions to these problems. However, if you choose to become very close to the person your child is dating, it is a good idea to reassure your son or daughter that your involvement is separate from their relationship:

> "Nancy, we do like Robb a great deal, and we feel sorry about his homelife, but we want to be sure that you understand a few things. First of all, no matter how much we like Robb, you are always first, and we will consider your wishes and feelings. If you ever feel that you would like to stop dating him for any reason, please be sure you do that. Don't feel hemmed in by our feelings for him."

A talk with Robb might go like this:

> "We care about you a great deal, but we don't want our involvement in your life to affect your decision about dating Nancy. If you ever decide to break up, it won't mean that we will never talk to you again. We will continue to like you. You must separate your relationship with Nancy from your relationship with us. Otherwise, it isn't good for any of us."

There are no easy solutions here. Be aware of the problems involved, get a feel for the situation, and make your decisions accordingly.

———

PORNOGRAPHY

Some parents are concerned when they find pornographic magazines, books, or pictures that belong to their adolescent. This is usually not a problem. Even if you find pornography distasteful, allow your son or daughter to have fairly normal adolescent fantasies. It isn't even suggested that you talk about what you have found. This will only embarrass your youngster for no good reason. It will also encourage lying to cover the embarrassment: "I'm just holding them for a friend until her mother has finished cleaning house."

There is another way in which teenagers try to make some sense out of a new and frequently confusing sexual identity. They may engage in very sexual conversations among themselves that parents overhear, or they may put their thoughts in notes or letters that parents find. Although there is a possibility that they are doing what they are talking about, the chances are that it is pure talk with little more substance than locker-room boasting. Today, such talk is as prevalent among young women as it is among young men.

It is likely that you will not appreciate what you see or hear, but it is not dangerous in itself. To take it literally or very seriously is a mistake that will only increase the tension at home.

If you hear the talk and don't like it, it is perfectly appropriate for you to state your opinion. But stating an opinion—even a very firm one—is far different from initiating a war of angry, frightened, self-righteous threats and put-downs.

LYING

There are basically three types of lying that teenagers engage in, and each one needs to be handled differently:

1. Lying to avoid revealing information that the adolescent feels is personal and need not be shared
2. Lying to avoid punishment or confrontation
3. Making up stories for no apparent reason

Lying to Avoid Revealing
Personal Information

Assume that your mother-in-law says, "Karen, do you and Ted fight a lot?" You and Ted do a fair amount of fighting, but you feel that it's none of her business. If you answer "yes," she will want to know what you fight about. If you say something like, "Now, Matilda, why would you want to know something like that?" she will tell you why she wants to know and continue the questioning. So to shut her up, you say "no."

Now, let's shift the generations. You ask your son Bill whether he's having any problems in school. Actually, Mr. Smith is driving him nuts in English because nothing Bill writes is good enough for Mr. Smith. But your son feels he can handle it just fine, so he says, "No, Ma." When Mr. Smith calls home the next day to say that Bill is in danger of flunking English, you accuse your son of lying: "I just asked you yesterday, and you said everything was fine. All I ask is that you tell me the truth. How can I ever trust you if I never know what's true?"

Your neighbor comes over and says, "Are you doing anything exciting tonight?" Actually, you are going out with another neighbor and definitely don't want this neighbor to come along. He is always trying to get himself invited to anything that's happening in the neighborhood. If you say you're not doing anything, he will invite himself over. If you say you're going out with the other neighbor, he will invite himself along, so you say, "Yes, we have to go to my sister-in-law's house tonight."

Your son comes home late from school, so you ask where he was. Actually, he had an argument with his girlfriend, and he was trying to talk some sense into her. It took so long that he missed the bus. And then a teacher found him in the hall and gave him a sermon about being late to class two days in a row. If there's anything your son doesn't want to do right now, it's go over the aggravating events of the last couple of hours, so he just says, "I stayed later to do homework."

Teenagers will also lie about other things that they feel is none of their parents' business. Whether it is the parents' business or not is not the question here. Adolescents have learned that in our society, it is acceptable to lie about things that are private and personal. Their list of private and personal things is very similar to an adult's list: sexual practices, minute details of work or school, details of conversations with friends, whereabouts, plans for the evening, etc.

The issue here is not lying. It is a different perception of what is the parents' business and what is not. Teenagers want to share only so much, and parents rarely feel that this is appropriate and sufficient. If a compromise is not possible, call your son or daughter stubborn, independent, obnoxious, or whatever you prefer, but don't call him or her a liar. This is not really an issue of truth or falsehood; it's an issue of privacy.

Lying to Avoid Punishment or Confrontation

"Who left these wet towels all over the bathroom floor?"

"Not me."

"Not me."

"Not me."

That leaves you, and you haven't used a towel today.

"Who broke the refrigerator door?"

"Who put mud prints all over my clean floor?"

"Did you go ice skating when I told you not to?"

"Did you drive the car over 70 miles an hour last night?"

It's hardly any wonder that no ones comes forward or tells the truth, but all those negative responses make you even madder.

There are really only two effective ways of dealing with such situations. The first is not to regularly ask questions that invite lying. The second is to make it a positive experience for your teenager to give you a truthful response:

"John, I do wish you would pick up after yourself more, but I really appreciate you honesty. Thank you!"

"Well, mud on the floor is fixable. Let's clean it up together. Thanks for being so honest. I like that in you."

"Please don't drive that car so fast. You will kill yourself and others. But, Mike, I do appreciate your honesty."

Making Up Stories

You have friends over and your daughter begins relating an exciting but totally false story. Later you overhear her tell a friend about an adventuresome vacation that she never took. Then she talks about an encounter with a teacher that is very questionable. Later in the week, she concocts a story about going to the movies with friends, when all she did was sit in the park. She tells kids at school about a rich and famous grandfather who doesn't exist.

Telling such tales is fairly common among small children; adolescents, however, should not share fantasies with others under the guise of truth. Repeated storytelling by age 15 or 16 needs some attention. There are more problems involved than the lying. The lying has a purpose and a function. Professional help should be sought so that this behavior will not continue into adulthood.

It does little or no good to punish teenagers for this type of storytelling. Occasionally the adolescent is really not sure where reality ends and fantasy begins. When such an adolescent relays an obvious lie, simply say, "We both know that isn't true. It might be nice if it were that way, but it just isn't."

It also isn't productive to humiliate your teenager in front of family or friends. It will not change the behavior. Seek professional help and follow the therapist's advice for dealing with your particular situation.

Chapter 3

Migraines

FRIENDS

When children are small, it is possible to keep them from having "undesirable" playmates. This practice is highly questionable at age 3, let alone at age 13. But with small children, it is within the realm of possibility. With adolescents, it is impossible. The more the parents forbid the teenager to have certain friends, the more "far out" the friends become.

If an adolescent is acting out, the parents' favorite scapegoat is the child's friends: "John is hanging around with the wrong crowd." It's amazing how many parents have sons or daughters who are helpless, pathetic followers. Very few have teenagers who instigate the wrongdoing. Since it is the friends who are to blame, the simplistic solution is to force a change in friends. The harder the parents insist on this, the worse the situation becomes. Parents are under the illusion that if the teenager's friends are different, he or she will be different. Usually, the opposite happens. As adolescents change, they find new friends.

What can parents do? They can work hard at building communication. A sermon is not communication. Parents can't change an adolescent's friends. Even moving to a different neighborhood or town doesn't help. The same friends (with different names) will appear on your doorstep within a week. Building communication about this problem can begin as follows:

Father: Jane, can we sit down and talk for a few minutes?

Jane: What did I do now?

Father: Nothing. I would just like to talk.

Jane: Sure, Dad. What's up?

Father: Could you tell me about your friends?

Jane: What do you mean?

Father: Just tell me about them—what they're really like and why you like them. Stuff like that.

Jane: Why do you want to know that?

Father: Oh, I don't know. I find myself not liking them sometimes, and I thought if you could talk about them, I'd get a more positive picture of what they're like.

Jane: I've always known you couldn't stand them.

Father: But if they're your friends, I *want* to like them. So help me out, please.

Jane: Well, actually, Dad, they aren't much to brag about. But I get so lonely, and I can't seem to make friends with nice kids. I just don't know what to do sometimes.

Father: I probably wouldn't know what to do either, but can we just talk about it? I may not have the answers, but I would like to listen. Maybe we can come up with something together.

Such a discussion is honest and is also very helpful and encouraging to a teenager. Friends are everything to a young person, but they are very difficult to make and even harder to keep.

As was stated earlier, the primary purpose of adolescence is to separate from parents. But this does not bring independence. The adolescent begins to lean heavily on the peer group instead of the parents for support and sustenance. However, all the young people in that peer group are going through the same problems, so the support is transient and precarious at best.

Your young adult needs these people badly, but there is always the danger that they will be gone tomorrow. That fear is real and sometimes paralyzing. Putting down a teenager's friends is like kicking a crutch away from a person with a broken foot.

Let us assume that you understand all this but are still very concerned about the young people who are hanging around your house. What are your objections? Do your teenager's friends look as if they are high most of the time, or do they just dress outlandishly? Friends who are distasteful to parents come in many varieties. If you fear heavy drug involvement, that is a serious problem; it is discussed later in this chapter and in Chapter 5. If your youngster's friends are well-known police problems and you have further evidence of illegal activity, that can be serious. But it is almost guaranteed that a change of scenery or a different set of friends will *not* change the real problem. Teenagers who have a drug problem or a problem that will land them in jail, for example, have underlying problems irrelevant to their friendships. Peer pressure can cause problems to surface, but the problems were there before.

What if your teenager's friends are just obnoxious, spoiled, poorly dressed, poor students, or otherwise unacceptable to you? This is not an area in which parents should interfere. They should trust their children enough to believe that they will either be a good influence on their friends or eventually get new friends.

It is important to remember that putting down the teenager's friends is putting the teenager down. It does no good for parents to say things like, "You are too good for them." That is not encouraging. It only convinces teenagers either that the parents don't know them or that they don't know their friends.

"I SAY BLACK; YOU SAY WHITE."

This describes a daily contest that can make the home into a war zone. It is something like the common cold. It is very uncomfortable, but basically harmless. However, without proper care, what seems like a cold can turn into pneumonia. Bickering can also become serious.

Everything the parent says is opposed. It goes something like this:

> *Mother:* Ann, could you close the door, please?
> *Ann:* Why are you always picking on me? You never ask Tom to close the door; only me.

> *Father:* It looks like rain.
> *Dave:* There you go again. You always look on the dark side of everything.

There is also the reverse:

> *Sarah:* Hi, Ma. How are you today?
> *Mother:* Don't talk so loud. I have a headache.

> *Pete:* Would you like me to mow the lawn?
> *Father:* It's about time you did something around here. When I was your age, I worked all day long.

The purpose of these oppositions is simply to argue, vie for power, or disparage the other person. This type of behavior on a periodic basis can also be due to a lot of tension in the individual's life. A 16-year-old can't yell at teachers, for example, so he or she may come home and yell at the parents instead. It's much safer. Parents also may react this way when things don't go well. A great deal of work is needed to reestablish cooperation and stop the put-downs. (See Chapters 8 to 10 for some assistance in this area.)

There are ways of reducing this behavior. As with most problems, the best way is to talk in a quiet, nonthreatening way. If there is a danger of yelling, go to a restaurant. Most people won't go into a rage in public.

Since the "I say black; you say white" model is usually a habit, it will be necessary to work on it with consistency:

1. Set a time to talk each week. The rules for talking are:
   (a) Use only "I" statements, that is, make no accusations. (See Chapter 9 for more details.)

    (b) Do not yell. Really listen to what your son or daughter is saying.

    (c) Find a private place to meet. If the situation has become very critical, a meeting should take place every day. Five minutes is sufficient.

2. Talk about one specific thing that each of you will work on. Don't try to change everything at once. Perhaps a father will agree to stop teasing his son about being uncoordinated, and the son will agree to say "hello" when he sees his father. They can agree on a signal to use if either one forgets. A nonverbal signal is usually good. A humorous one is even better. Scratching the head, stretching the arms, winking, or sending any other nonthreatening signal is acceptable. It is obviously not good to make any verbal responses such as, "You forgot." An accusation or anything close to an accusation will only start an argument.

Reducing negative statements and behaviors is essential, but it is even better if one of the fighting parties can find a nice, positive thing to say to the other. (See Chapters 8 to 12 for more details on communication.)

Without this reorientation to the positive, love, respect, and affection will be absent or difficult to reestablish. If it's a one-sided endeavor, so what?

> **The only person you can be sure of changing is yourself.**

Although mother-daughter and father-son wars are the most common, any combination is possible. One of the worst possible combinations is that of one parent and one child who team up against the other parent.

A typical scenario involves one parent who is a great listener. He or she is kind, understanding, and positive. The teenager feels loved and understood. Wonderful. The only problem is that all the son's or daughter's confidences are directed against the other parent. The "kind" parent becomes an ally against the "mean" parent. This is a devastating triangle that is common but unhealthy. The kind parent may also talk of divorce—to the child, not the spouse—as a way to save the child. What can be done to change such a situation?

1. Seek marriage counseling to repair your relationship with your spouse. If he or she won't go, go yourself to get some perspective on the situation and support for change.
2. Tell your teenager that you will no longer side with him or her against the other parent and that you also won't keep secrets from the other parent. End forever the teenager's admonition, "Don't tell Dad" or "Don't tell Mom."
3. Continue to be kind, supportive, and positive, but not at the expense of your spouse.
4. When your son or daughter begins to complain about the other parent, kindly suggest that he or she talk to the other parent about it.

Initially your adolescent will be very hurt and angry at this change in role. What is really happening in this perverse triangle is that the "good" parent and the "abused" child are parenting the other parent. I would feel very upset if, as an adult parent, I suddenly found myself being treated like a child again. A teenager living in the home is not a parent and should not assume or be given that status in any way, shape, or form.

SEX AND THE THIRD DEGREE

Usually the third degree involves parental questions related to sex and drugs. The questions are asked firmly or angrily, they are usually construed by the adolescent as a put-down, and they rarely deal directly with the issue of concern.

Parents who are worried about a teenager's sexual involvement will not say, "We want you home by eleven o'clock because we don't want you making out in the car after you go to the movie." What many will say instead is, "I want you home by eleven o'clock because I'm the parent and those are my rules. I don't care if all your friends get in at one."

More typical is the third-degree format:

Father: Where were you?
Daughter: At Tim's house.
Father: Were his parents home?
Daughter: Yes.
Father: Why did you go to his house?
Daughter: We had no money and it was too cold in the car.
Father: Why didn't you come here?
Daughter: Because you sit next to us all evening.
Father: Well, where do his parents sit?

There would be a lot less pain, agony, and confusion if this father expressed his real feelings. For example:

> "Since you've been going out with Tim, I've been worried about the amount of sexual activity in your relationship. I know that probably sounds dumb or square—whatever you want to call it. But I can't make the fear go away, no matter how hard I try. I care about you so much; I just don't want to see you get hurt. Heavy sexual involvement is difficult to handle. I'm just worried about that."

That is something your son or daughter can deal with.

The fact is that many adolescents have sexual intercourse before the age of 20. There is little way of knowing whether your teenager will or will not. Parents must remember that premarital sex is much more common among adolescents today than it was twenty years ago.

Teenagers who lead an active sex life are not usually promiscuous, and they do not feel that what they are doing is immoral. Many older teenagers handle a sexual involvement very well; some do not. But that can be said about almost anything in an adolescent's life. Some handle responsibility well; some do not. Some handle school well; some do not.

But if parents feel strongly that premarital sex is wrong or harmful, worrying about their teenager can become debilitating. Parents feel helpless, and this very helplessness can lead to damaging fights and distrust. So what are parents to do?

Parents fall into one of three basic categories when it comes to the question of premarital sex:

1. Those who believe that it is morally wrong and must be avoided.
2. Those who believe that it is not morally wrong but who feel that it is a heavy emotional burden during adolescence.
3. Those who are not particularly concerned one way or the other.

Whatever position you hold, it is important to maintain communication. Adolescents profit from an opportunity to talk about sex with their parents. Respectful, honest talking and listening are the only chance parents have to influence their children's lives positively in this area. More important, however, listening is critical in helping your son or daughter sort out the pressures, feelings, and confusion that are part of growing up today.

When adolescents begin dating, the parents can talk with them about the feelings on both sides. It is best not to sermonize, prohibit sexual behavior, or lecture. All that gets you is a verbal assent to your wishes, after which the teenager does as he or she pleases. The following is a statement, made by a father to his son, that is guaranteed to have a much greater impact than a sermon:

"I know there are many pressures on teenagers to have sex. Your mother and I don't approve of sex before marriage, so of course we hope you won't do it. It isn't that we just feel it's immoral; we also feel it's a lot of responsibility. Sex is for adults, but having sex doesn't make you an adult any more than smoking or swearing does. However, I am your father—not your judge or your conscience. The only thing I really ask is that you not do anything to hurt yourself or another person. If you must have sex, be sure the two of you use more than an adequate amount of birth control."

Another alternative is to say:

"I don't feel that sex before marriage is bad, but I do feel that sex demands maturity and a responsibility to the other person. Could we talk about that a little?"

The point is that parents should state their position on the issue and allow their children to do likewise. This shows caring and great respect for the young adult. Parents need not change their ideas to "go along with the times" or for any other reason. It's just that forbidding, judging, and yelling at your adolescent are surefire ways to cause yourself problems.

Parents can often handle the issue of premarital sex without a great deal of difficulty, albeit with some uneasiness and hesitancy and a fair amount of worry. What happens, however, if you find your daughter's birth control pills? Do you rant and rave? Do you make believe you didn't find them? Do you forbid her to see her boyfriend again? Do you ban her boyfriend from the house?

The very first thing to do is *nothing!* Leave the pills where you found them and give yourself plenty of time to calm down. Talk to a trusted friend; do anything that will give you some time to get a perspective on the matter. It is very important to calm down before making a decision about what to do.

Once you are as calm as you feel you will ever be about the situation, it is important to look at how you found the pills. If you were searching in her dresser, that was not appropriate; however, it is done, and you must think about what to do now. If you decide to talk to your daughter about what you found, begin by apologizing for snooping. Say that you know it wasn't the right thing to do, but you did it, and now you would like to discuss what you found. Please don't yell! I can almost guarantee that it will not change her sexual behavior. All it can do is drive her away when she needs you the most. Let her talk. Express your opinion without putting her down. Agree to disagree if necessary, but talk quietly and in a reassuring manner. Above all, do not bring the incident up later to put her down. Let it die. Don't risk driving her away.

If you decide not to talk to her about it, you must feel very confident that you can forget about what you found because if you can't, you will react to her in a negative way without her knowing why. In such a situation, a mother or father tends to have an all-knowing attitude:

"Be sure your boyfriend doesn't come in the house while we're gone."

"Why not?"

"Don't ask me, 'Why not?' Do you think I was born yesterday? I know what you're doing, and I won't allow it."

Such an attitude will confuse your daughter since she has no idea that you have found the pills.

But what if the pills were left on top of the dresser for all to see? Although your daughter may not have been entirely aware of her intentions, it is a good bet that she "accidentally" left them for you to find. In the words of a 16-year-old:

> "I know Mom probably knows I'm sleeping with Bob, but I think she's afraid to talk to me about it. She doesn't want to yell at me, but she doesn't want it to seem as if she approves either. I just don't know. I want to talk to her about it so badly, but I'm scared of how she will react. She doesn't have to approve. I just don't want her to make a scene or something. She really understands a lot. But I'm afraid to find out if she will understand this."

This is the girl who will be careless and leave the pills for her mother to find. She probably feels somewhat confused and guilty, and she may be wondering whether she should continue her sexual behavior. Or she may have decided that this behavior is fine, but she would like to talk about it with her mother in an adult way. This girl deserves special kindness and understanding.

There is another type of discovery that is a little more difficult to deal with. What happens when you walk in on your teenager and a boyfriend or girlfriend while they are in partial or total state of undress? Your ability to handle crises will determine how you react more than anything else. It would be nice if you could calmly ask them to get dressed and meet you in the kitchen for a quiet discussion. But let's face it; there is only so much a parent can be expected to do. What will probably happen is that you will rant and rave, scaring the pair out of at least two years' growth. After this initial emotional outburst, it would be good to get away from the situation and calm down; then return for a reasonable discussion. Whether you approve of premarital sex or not, try to put what happened in perspective. It is not the end of the world.

When you do have your discussion, remember the suggestions for dealing with a teenager's sexual involvement given earlier in the chapter. State your views, set limits about the use of your home, and do whatever else is necessary in light of your opinions. Just don't disparage the ill-fated lovers; don't make your son or daughter feel rejected or too terrible to deserve your love. Parents can never assume that children know they are loved, no matter what happens. They don't.

> ***Children need to be constantly reminded that they are loved, especially when parents are denouncing their actions.***

It is difficult to communicate displeasure without communicating rejection in circumstances like this.

You may wonder: "I've communicated; I've been loving and understanding. Now how do I get them to stop?" I hate to tell you this, but there are no authoritarian ways to stop a teenager's sexual behavior. Once a couple begin sleeping together, the chances of getting them to stop by forbidding them to do it are very slim indeed. They will just be more careful not to get caught. The only chance you have of changing the behavior is to remain open to discussion.

There is another interesting side to the coin. Some parents want to be liberal and "with it." They don't overreact; they know the score and want to be sure their adolescents are aware of their understanding and support. They buy their children birth control devices prior to the first date and encourage them to talk about their sexual encounters. They act more like the adolescent's peers than like parents. This is very confusing to teenagers, even if they profess to appreciate the help and openness.

First of all, some adolescents are not ready for sexual activity, and parents such as these add to the monumental pressures that are already there. Second, adolescents want their parents to set boundaries—not to forbid certain behavior but to set boundaries. They also need to see their parents as older, wiser, and a little more conservative than they are (whether they are or not). Otherwise, parents have little more credibility than a 16-year-old. Parents provide a needed security that friends do not. When parents become friends with their children—peers—the confusion that results can be detrimental.

RELIGION

Adolescents whose parents are religious may refuse to go to church or temple. They may casually suggest that God does not exist. The alarmed parents seek help from their priest, minister, or rabbi, who then talks to the son or daughter. An enlightened religious leader will pull out of the fight and encourage the parents to do likewise. However, most oblige the parents by going to the adolescent with pleas, threats, and admonitions. This just serves to intensify a battle that need not be fought.

Again it is important that parents tell their son or daughter how they feel and what they think, but it is counterproductive to make church attendance the cause of a battle.

There is no question that this can be an extremely painful experience, especially for parents who are deeply committed to their religion. There is little that anyone can say to reduce the pain if parents sincerely believe that such a form of rebellion is akin to spiritual suicide.

But coercion rarely works, and a massive fight reduces the chances that the adolescent will return to the parents' religion. On the other hand, pulling out of the fight (especially with younger teenagers) frequently results in renewed church attendance within six months to a year. With older teenagers, it may take two or three years, or the adolescent may never return to church.

Changing religions is another form of rebellion or personal choice that can cause very serious problems and a great deal of turmoil. Parents see it as a way of being told, "Your values stink. I reject what is important to you. Get out of my

life." In their search for identity, many adolescents have to give
that message. Most of them do it more kindly, but separation
from parents initially demands more force than many parents
can accept without suffering.

If the parents are very religious and their teenager rejects
their religion, pain is inevitable, but a breakdown in communication is not. This must be avoided. A good way to handle the
situation is as follows:

Parent: You are really too old for us to drag you to
church. We were terribly upset after you told us
you didn't believe in God, but you are our son no
matter what. Of course, we would prefer it if you
came to church with us, but we don't want to
force you. What we would like to do now, though,
is really sit and listen to you. Our anger has sub-
sided, so we would like to hear how you came to
this decision. We will try very hard not to argue or
get mad. We just want to listen.

Frank: Thank you. Actually, I don't know if I believe in
God or not. It's just all so confusing that I don't
know what to do. Sometimes I stay awake nights
trying to figure it all out. But nothing seems to
help.

Parent: That must be scary sometimes.

Frank: Oh, it is. One night I woke up in a cold sweat.
Sometimes you have really shoved religion down
my throat, you know—no offense. I mean I just
accepted it for so many years without really giving
it any thought. Then all of a sudden, I started
noticing that religious people are often very rotten
to other people. They go to church on Sunday and
knock everybody down the rest of the week. It's
kind of sickening, really.

Parent: It's true that does happen. We do that too sometimes, so it must be even more confusing for you.

Frank: No, I didn't mean you. It's just all so crazy somehow. I can't figure it out. Part of me stopped going

to church because it doesn't make sense anymore;
but I know part of me stopped because I wanted to
tell you that I can't accept things just because you
do. I don't really want to hurt you. I just can't be
you. Can you understand that?

Parent: Part of us can and part of us can't, I suppose.

Frank: All I ask is for you to try, because this is a hell of a
time for me. I need to know you still care for me
even though I'm making choices that I know hurt
you.

There is also another side to the issue of religion. If the
parents are nonreligious or atheistic, the young adult may try
to find the most conservative denomination around and accept
it with the fervor of Joan of Arc.

The pain of seeing one's child flaunt such basic parental
values is as great for nonreligious parents as it is for the most
religious. The problem and the anxiety are very similar: "I
tried hard to instill values that I think are important, and this
16-year-old kid stands there and tells me that he knows more
about life, more about what is important, than I do. How can I
save him from this fate? Where did I go wrong? This just can't
happen to my son!"

ALCOHOL AND DRUG USE

Occasional use of marijuana or alcohol during the middle or
later teenage years is not cause for major concern. It happens
frequently. That does not mean that parents should approve of
the behavior or encourage it; it means that the behavior should
be kept in perspective.

Parents have two major questions related to occasional alcohol or drug use: (1) Should they allow their teenagers to
drink at home? (2) How should they handle it if their son or
daughter comes home drunk or high?

Use of alcohol in the home is so closely tied to cultural and

occasionally religious differences, as well as to parental prefer-
ences, that it is difficult to make flat statements that apply to
everyone. Generally speaking, however, allowing teenagers to
have a beer or a glass of wine occasionally may be appropriate.
However, beer or other alcoholic beverages should generally
not be available for frequent consumption. Special holidays or
celebrations are enough.

Allowing or even encouraging adolescents to drink at
home does not mean that they will drink less at parties, in a
friend's car, or in the forest preserve. Although there are many
exceptions, the more teenagers drink at home, the greater the
possibility that they will overuse alcohol somewhere else. Drinking at home does not satisfy teenagers' curiosity about drinking
or lessen their desire to drink too much. Drinking at home
makes drinking elsewhere easier.

If your son or daughter comes home drunk, it won't do
much good to yell and carry on. The next day, however, it is
helpful to ask your teenager to explain his or her behavior.
Listen carefully. Encourage talking about anything that comes
up. Did he or she go out planning to get drunk? For what
reason? Pressure? Boredom? To be like everyone else? To see
what it was like? Or did your adolescent get drunk to forget
problems? Perhaps your son or daughter hadn't planned on
getting drunk, but the drinks tasted so good that he or she just
didn't stop.

If your teenager gets drunk because he or she likes the
taste and just keeps drinking, you probably have a problem. It's
almost certain that the taste was developed as a result of a lot of
previous drinking. If your adolescent wanted to get drunk to
forget about some problems, put the drinking aside for a minute and ask about the problems. Drinking to forget is a very
dangerous pattern.

Occasionally male teenagers are almost encouraged to get
drunk once in a while, especially by their fathers. The verbal
message to the young man might be to avoid excessive drinking, but the subtle, underlying message is that "tying one on" is
masculine and expected. "He's really growing up, I guess," one
father related with some pride after a school official called to

tell him that his son was very intoxicated at a school dance. If a teenage boy gets adulthood and masculinity confused with drinking, he and his parents are in for some difficult times.

Another very serious issue related to alcohol and other drug use is driving while high or intoxicated. When your son or daughter gets a license, it is suggested that you have a discussion similar to the following:

> "We do not approve of your drinking or using any other drugs. However, if you ever do get high or drunk, be very sure that you do not drive the car. Call us in the middle of the night if necessary, and we will come to pick you up or let you stay overnight. We will not yell and carry on. Drinking is serious, but death is worse. If you have a ride with someone else who is drunk or high, call us. We will talk to you about the incident the next day, but without anger or punishment.
>
> We are very serious about this, and we want you to know that if you ever drive while you are high or drunk, you will not drive again for six months."

Obviously, if you make such a rule for your teenager, you have to be a parent who never drives while drunk or high either. You also have to be very sure that you can follow through on what you have said:

1. You must not become angry (or show your anger) when you go to pick up your son or daughter at 1 A.M.
2. If your son or daughter drives while drunk, whatever consequence was established earlier must be carried out to the letter. If you said that your son couldn't drive for three months, you must not allow him to drive for three months, even if the prom is next week. He will have to get a ride with someone else, call a cab, or do whatever else is necessary to get to the prom without your car (or his own, if he has one).

Promise only what you can deliver, whether it is positive or negative.

And what about use of other drugs? The problems with other drugs are similar to the problems with alcohol; in addition, other drugs are illegal, and therefore it is difficult for teenagers to know exactly what they are getting. A third problem is that parents are less familiar with other drugs and therefore tend to react more negatively to them. Marijuana, cocaine, and amphetamines are not good, but neither is alcohol. It is not better if your children drink instead of using other drugs. It is just as bad.

In this section, we are discussing occasional use—not overuse or addiction. Although many high school students use drugs or alcohol on a regular basis for recreational purposes, that does not mean that this behavior should be approved or condoned. It also does not mean that you should do nothing if your adolescent comes home drunk or high many more times than you can tolerate. Trust is better than vigilance any day, but if, after repeated incidents of drunkenness, trust no longer exists, there are some steps that you can take, short of grounding your son or daughter for life:

1. If your teenager is going to a party, call the parents to verify that a party is being held and to be assured that no alcohol will be served and that no other drugs will be allowed. Be sure you know where the party is taking place. Ask whether the parents will be present during the entire evening.
2. Be sure you know how your adolescent is getting to the party and how he or she is getting home, as well as at what time.
3. If your son or daughter has come home drunk or high many times before, you may ask that you be awakened when he or she gets home.
4. If your teenager is giving a party, make it clear that you will not tolerate alcohol or drugs. If someone brings in alcohol or drugs, ask that person to leave.
5. If possible, don't have the party in a separate part of the house. You need to be able to walk through the room

where the party is going on as unobtrusively as possible many times.

6. Do not have large parties. They are almost impossible to control. If you relent in spite of this warning, inform the police that you are having a large party. You may need their assistance later in the evening. They may also come over at the request of neighbors who can't take the noise one minute longer.

_____*Chapter 4*_____

School Problems

Although some school problems are not serious, in most cases they are much more serious than any of the problems discussed in the last three chapters.

"I hate school. I'm getting out as soon as I can." When an adolescent makes a statement like this, parents become frightened, and educators are threatened. Occasionally that is the sole purpose of the statement. There are basically three types of "I hate school" adolescents:

1. Those who act out by failing or by doing more poorly than it is reasonable to expect, for any of the following reasons:
   (a) To get attention or establish a place in the family
   (b) To wake parents up to problems
   (c) To "get" the parents (revenge)
   (d) To cover up feelings of inadequacy
2. Those who work hard, but in nonproductive ways
3. Those who become school phobics

THE FAILING STUDENT

In most school systems, students do not fail unless they really work at it. They have to skip a lot of classes, avoid doing homework, not study for tests, and generally communicate in other ways the need for an F.

Since school failure is more serious than most of the problems discussed earlier, it is important for parents to take it seriously without overreacting. A panic response on the parents' part can make the problem much worse. Let's look more closely at the motives for failing. A better understanding of school problems can frequently help you respond better.

Motive 1: To get attention

Every child in the family needs a "place." If one or more children are very good students, that place is taken. Poor performance has much more potential for getting attention. Parents can be extremely attentive when trying to motivate a child to be a better student. Negative attention is not necessarily bad in the teenager's eyes. It is certainly much better than no attention or less attention than is desired.

The only way to change this behavior is to stop giving the child attention for nonperformance and to increase positive attention. See Chapter 10 for specific suggestions.

Motive 2: To communicate that a problem is present

The problem is rarely clear-cut and is frequently difficult or impossible for the adolescent to articulate. In other words, just asking your son or daughter what the problem is will probably not help. The problem can be related to a fear of growing up, anxiety about choosing a career, a lack of friends, etc. The problem might also have to do with a more obvious situation in the teenager's life, such as an impending divorce, insecurity about there not being enough money in the family, the death of a parent or grandparent, or a fear of having to move to another town and/or go to another school. In some cases, problems in school result when a pet dies or when a close friend moves away. The list of possibilities is very long indeed.

If your son or daughter has a problem with school, contact the school counselor, psychologist, or social worker; these people may know the young adult well enough to provide some direction for you. That's a good place to begin. The teenager may be happy to see one of these people on a regular basis, but would not have initiated the contact on his or her own.

Sometimes it is best to seek help outside the school system. Short-term help, given soon after the problem arises, can frequently prevent more serious problems from developing later. But it is also possible that things will turn around by themselves before too long. See Chapter 6 for suggestions about what to do if improvement doesn't occur within a reasonable period.

Motive 3: To get revenge

If the purpose of the school failure is to "get" the parents, usually the teenager develops a consistent pattern of behavior that keeps the parents involved all semester. The route taken depends on school policy.

For instance, if the school calls home each time a student skips a class, the adolescent who seeks power or revenge will skip on a periodic basis. If the school sends notices home when homework is not handed in, the teenager will fail to do homework just long enough to get the notices sent home. From the adolescent's point of view, this is much more effective than doing no homework at all or not going to school at all, which might tend to make parents and teachers give up. This would not gratify the student. He or she must keep the adults in a constant state of stress and agitation in order to get maximum satisfaction.

The best thing the parents can do is to *pull out of the fight!* When the school failure no longer serves its purpose—namely, to aggravate the parents—it will be discontinued or replaced by a more effective tool. Families at this level of noncommunication may need some outside help to rebuild a deteriorating relationship. However, pulling out of the fight and making real efforts at understanding the purpose of the behavior may solve the problem.

Jane, an angry 14-year-old, talks with her counselor after getting three F's on her report card:

Counselor:	What's the payoff when you get F's?
Jane (laughing):	My father yells till the veins bulge in his neck. My mother cries and pulls at her hair. It's really quite a scene!
Counselor:	Can you think of any other ways you might get your anger out? Does it *have* to come out at them in this way?
Jane:	Absolutely! I owe them; boy, do I owe them. And failing is the only way I can really get them.

This situation is obviously out of hand, but nothing will improve in that family until the parents change their behavior. And they are so angry that they refuse to change: "Let her get F's; that will fix her." Unfortunately, Jane is a hundred miles away from being "fixed." She doesn't even want to separate from her parents. She wants to hang around and torture them—and she does it very well. As long as her parents allow this to continue, nothing will change. The point is that they are allowing themselves to be tortured. If Jane can no longer make them suffer, her vicious game will be over. The solution is simple if not easy—her parents must pull out of the fight.

How do they do that? A starting point is to state their case simply. Jane's mother or father can say:

"There is no way we can make you go to your classes or do your homework. We deliver you to the front door of the school, and you leave by the back. We make you sit at your desk, but you don't study. It is no longer our responsibility. It is all yours. We are not going to hassle you about it anymore. And we will not accept responsibility for it."

In practical terms, what does all this mean? It means if you are involved in a situation like this, you should not set hours for studying or even ask about homework, and you should not ground your son or daughter when notices come home. You should be pleasant and supportive, but you must not become involved in getting your teenager to pass.

When failure notices come home, simply give them to your son or daughter and quietly and pleasantly say, "Mary, these are addressed to us, but they are for you. I am confident you can take care of them." If the school calls home, leave a note for Mary saying: "Mary, the school called me today, but I said that only you can handle this. I was told that you skipped three classes. I assume you know that, but I just wanted to leave the message in case there is an error."

If your adolescent is not doing better in school within six months to a year, seek professional help. But in many cases, a reversal in parental overinvolvement results in a reversal in school performance. The biggest problem parents have is changing their reactions and their basic outlook. Unfortunately, the school doesn't always offer a lot of help. Teachers and administrators are frustrated when your child does not achieve up to his or her capacity, so they call you in the hope that you will succeed where they have failed. You may sense disapproval for being "remiss in your duties."

But even if teachers and administrators realize that the teenager—not the parents—must handle the problem, they may feel obligated to make parents aware when a student skips classes or performs poorly. To be aware is one thing, but to be responsible is quite another. Accept the calls from the school as information, but not as directives to become more involved or otherwise assume responsibility for your child's actions.

There are also different levels of overprotection and overinvolvement. Moderately overprotective parents blame themselves: "Where did we go wrong?" They try to assume responsibility for their son or daughter. Extremely overprotective parents blame everyone else:

"The teacher is out to get my little darling."

"The attendance office is totally inept and makes a lot of mistakes."

"No one at school cares whether children learn or not."

"The classes are boring."

"The teacher yells at him."

"His friends are a bad influence."

"The dog ate her homework."

If you recognize such overprotectiveness in yourself, you should concentrate hard on changing your outlook and behavior. Overprotection hampers normal adolescent growth. Only physical and psychological neglect, cruelty, and inconsistency are worse.

Children need love, support, encouragement, attention, and time, but they do not need parents to do for them what they should do for themselves.

Motive 4: To cover up feelings of inadequacy

If "success"—especially in school—is a strong family value, an average student who feels unable to measure up will begin skipping school or failing to do homework and then blame the failure or lower grades on these actions. Parents and others can say, "If you tried, you could get an A." The teenager *knows* that he or she cannot get an A without cheating and decides that it is better to be considered irresponsible than inadequate.

In such a situation, the most obvious first step is to remove the pressure for superior performance. That is much easier said than done, however. A good person to question is the high school counselor. Ask how well your son or daughter is expected to be doing. If C's are expected for the courses he or she is taking, try sitting down and discussing the issue. A remarkable improvement in school performance and in general psychological health can take place when a parent talks in the following manner:

> "I spoke to your counselor at school today and to a couple of your teachers. I found out I've been really unfair. They said that you're working hard and that perhaps I'm pushing you too much. You do the best you can in school, and I shouldn't expect all A's. I'm sorry for placing that pressure on you. You are so creative and so intuitive that I just assumed it was my obligation to push you to do the very best. I just didn't believe you when you said you were doing your best. I'm sorry about that."

Listen to a 16-year-old discussing school with his counselor:

> "I know I could get a few A's, but I have to be careful not to. Let's say I get straight A's this semester; if I end up with two B's next semester, I'll get grounded or yelled at for doing so poorly. Sometimes I won't hand in an assignment just so I can avoid getting an A. I can't take the pressure of getting all A's all the time."

A 14-year-old girl had this to say about her poor grades:

> "What would you do if you had my name? Two brothers and a sister have gone through this school before me. Two were valedictorians, and one was a National Merit winner. No way I'm going to get stuck in that mess. Caroline didn't have a date till she got to college. Study, study, study all day and all night. It's sickening. Anyhow, what is there left for me to win? Who can top what they've already done? The only way I've ever been able to get any attention in that house is to fail. I'm beginning to worry, though, that I won't be able to get a job if I don't shape up pretty soon. But I just can't stand being mediocre or ignored. It's humiliating."

THE STUDENT WHO WORKS HARD BUT GETS NOWHERE

Such a student can sit at a desk for three hours but actually spend about five minutes studying. Daydreaming, guilt feelings, and depression are common among students like this. The most typical student in this category is again one who cannot handle parental overprotection. A 16-year-old girl explained her problem to her counselor as follows:

> *Counselor:* Sandy, what happens when you go home?
> *Sandy:* I'm tired, so I put the TV on and sit down. Then my mother asks me if I have homework. Of course I do, but I want to relax for a minute.

Counselor: What happens next?

Sandy: I feel guilty watching TV when I've got homework, so I go upstairs to study, but I end up just staring. I can't concentrate.

Counselor: How do you feel at that point?

Sandy: Hopeless.

Counselor: What happens next?

Sandy: My father comes home, we eat dinner, and then he sits next to me to help me with my homework. Sometimes he checks over homework I've already done and finds mistakes. Then I really want to give up. So I usually just let him do it. I'm responsible. I do the best I can. But when he sits there and checks everything, it's just not my work anymore, so I don't care. I would rather get a D on my own than my father's B. He makes me feel like a stupid little kid, but he's so nice to me that I don't want to hurt him.

A useful rule of thumb is that if a teenager asks for help with homework, the parents should provide some, but they should let the teenager assume responsibility for school.

Adolescents may also do poorly in school for reasons unrelated to overprotectiveness. The signal is that they begin getting lower grades while studying the same amount of time. Lack of concentration is the biggest problem. There is also a loss of motivation and displeasure with past goals. All of us are depressed or unhappy at certain times. However, if this persists for longer than normal, the parent should seek help. See Chapter 6 for a more detailed discussion.

Failure or reduced performance is not the only problem. Some students may just have a hard time with school or consistently find some subjects particularly difficult. What can parents do to help?

1. Encourage your adolescent to suggest his or her own solutions. Is it a problem for him or just for you? If it's

more your worry than his, most solutions you try won't work.

2. Talk to your child's teachers to find out the nature of the problem and get their suggestions.

3. Inquire about tutoring at school or private tutoring. If your adolescent is receptive to this, it will help. If he or she resents it, it will make matters worse.

THE PHOBIC STUDENT

The phobic student refuses to go to school. He or she may have severe anxiety attacks when approaching the school building or individual classrooms. A more common way of staying away is to claim illness. Parents frequently cooperate in the sham by calling the school to say the child is sick.

Any student who misses an inordinate amount of school because of vague physical complaints or anxiety can be considered a school phobic. Professional psychological help should be sought. This is not a do-it-yourself project, and the problem usually will not go away on its own. It will only get worse.

All the problems discussed in this chapter are possible reasons for school failure or poor performance. However, sudden loss of interest in school, resulting in lower grades, is frequently caused by drug and/or alcohol abuse. Chapter 5 provides more information on this problem.

When Self-Help Won't Do It

Communication, cooperation, mutual respect, and sometimes getting tough can work wonders even with difficult family problems. Such self-help approaches can improve the situation and help restore harmony to the family. But there are times when self-help alone just won't change things around and when outside psychological help is necessary. It is important for parents to know when that point has been reached. This chapter discusses the more common signs.

SOCIAL PROBLEMS

An almost total lack of friends on a consistent basis may be a cause for concern. It may also be a matter of circumstances or personality. It is a fairly common occurrence, however, so don't be overly concerned unless there is further evidence of problems. More serious things to look for include manipulation of others for favors without any effort to reciprocate and a lack of concern for the feelings, wishes, and well-being of others. Appropriate feelings of guilt or remorse may be absent.

Excessively aggressive behavior is a more obvious reason for concern. This might include a pattern of fighting, stealing, committing acts of vandalism, or setting fires. Unfortunately, far too many parents refuse to heed such obvious signs of trouble.

A 14-year-old boy had initiated four fights in two weeks, had sworn at a teacher, and had been caught throwing a small bomb into a garbage can inside the school. His father stormed into the principal's office with fire in his eyes and in front of his son said, "How dare you pull me away from work for nothing! He's a growing boy. What did you do when you were his age—play ring-around-the-rosy?"

This boy was a very angry young man, but in addition he was following his father's dictum about appropriate masculine behavior. Unless there is a meaningful intervention, such adolescents have a very good chance of spending some or a lot of time in prison. Even if they do avoid going to prison, the chances that they will have good social relationships are very slim.

Another student admitted that he had extorted hundreds of dollars from other students by threatening to beat them up. Those who refused to pay were beaten up. His mother's response: "I guess boys will be boys."

Many specifically aggressive behaviors may occur in conjunction with other symptoms—drug abuse, out-of-control behavior, agitated depression, etc. The purpose here is not to diagnose or categorize, but simply to list as many danger signals as possible. Parents should know when outside intervention is needed. If there is a question in your mind, discuss it with others. But don't allow consistent problem behavior to continue without making some attempt at intervention. Early help can often mean earlier and shorter recovery.

EATING DISORDERS

Anorexia Nervosa

This is a disorder most common among adolescent girls. It usually starts with successful dieting—hardly an unusual phenomenon. The trouble begins when the girl (and in rare cases, the boy) becomes very thin, even by today's standards, and continues to diet with almost religious fervor. She may say that she feels and looks fat, when everyone around her is startled by her emaciated appearance. She becomes preoccupied with her body size and is often found staring into a mirror. She may also prepare elaborate meals for others, but eat little or nothing herself.

The anorexic girl often becomes irritated by parental concerns. She does not believe she has a problem, so she is resistant to therapy.

Anorexic behavior definitely signals the need for therapeutic intervention. Medical attention may also be necessary. In severe cases, hospitalization is required to replace certain body chemicals that have been lost as well as to provide enough calories to sustain life. In rare cases, death from starvation results.

Bulimia

Bulimia is a binge-and-purge disorder. The binge involves consumption of a great deal of food very quickly. The food consumed is usually sweet and high in calories. The binge frequently ends with self-induced vomiting. The purge, as well as the binge, may be pelasurable in many cases.

Unlike anorexics, bulimics realize that their eating is not normal, and therefore depression and a fear of losing all control follow a binge episode.

Bulimics are almost always women, and the disorder usually begins in adolescence or early adulthood. Some have weight fluctuations due to alternating binges and fasts, and a good number use laxatives in addition to inducing vomiting. Most are within a normal weight range, while a few are underweight or overweight.

Although bulimia is not normally life-threatening, dehydration and electrolyte imbalance are possible consequences.

After a number of years, those who vomit frequently also lose the enamel on the underside of their teeth.

Bulimia is a symptom of serious psychological problems and should be taken very seriously. However, neither medication nor therapy can provide a quick cure.

SEXUAL TRAUMA

Rape

Rape can have a severe and lasting impact on any woman, young or old. Therapy is not always indicated, but some short-term counseling is usually helpful. In many cities there are support groups for women who have been raped. Remember, too, that the effects of the trauma frequently do not become apparent until much later.

Incest

The victims of incest almost always require therapy, some for a very long time. Generally speaking, the earlier the sexual contact began and the longer it lasted, the worse the scars are.

Incest is defined here as any sexual activity with a close relative—a parent, stepparent, brother, or uncle, for example. It can range from fondling to sexual intercourse, and the behavior usually progresses in that way over time if it is not detected and stopped. The most serious form of incest is that involving a child and a parent or stepparent. Brother-sister incest does not seem to have as severe a psychological impact.

The degree of cooperation on the part of the child does not significantly affect the amount of damage that results. Incest is frequently not rape. The child may cooperate with the parent or other person and in some cases may even enjoy the attention. But this increases the psychological trauma. It doesn't make it any easier on the child.

There is another disturbing fact about incest. When the story finally is told to someone outside the family, the victim invariably says that the mother (or occasionally the father, in the case of mother-son incest) was told what was happening and dismissed or ignored the report. This makes the problem even worse.

There are also many misconceptions about incest. First, it is not confined to the lower socioeconomic classes. It happens as frequently in very rich families as in very poor ones. Second, the guilty person is usually not sent to jail unless someone presses charges, and even then convictions are rare. This depends largely, however, on the state in which the incestuous relationship takes place and on current public opinion. It is commonly accepted that jail is not the answer in 95 percent of cases of incest anyway. Intensive therapy for the entire family is much more appropriate.

What do you do if you find out about incest in your family? You should find a therapist who has experience in this area. Just as many therapists are not trained to work with adolescents, many are not trained to work with families in which incest is a problem. If you are too embarrassed to identify yourself, you can call various places anonymously.

Public agencies almost always have someone on the staff who can provide services. For a private referral, you might try psychiatric hospitals or hospitals with a psychiatric section. It is also possible to call a branch of the American Psychological Association in your city or the nationwide number—(202) 833-7600—and ask for the name of psychologists in your area who have experience with this problem. You can also call the national child abuse hotline and ask for a referral. The number is (216) 696-5437.

Although state laws differ, generally speaking, whomever you eventually contact is bound by law to report the abuse to the Department of Children and Family Services or its equivalent. Nothing else need happen as long as you follow through with therapy. If you have any questions about the laws and practices in your state, ask the therapist or agency that you contact.

However, you must do *something*. Do not dismiss the situation. Some mothers have said they thought their daughters were lying. Even if it is a lie, there is something radically wrong if your daughter is making up that kind of story. Whether it is true or not, there is a serious problem. Take it seriously and do something, or you will compound the problem.

DEPRESSION

The usual signs of depression include insomnia, oversleeping, waking early, a low energy level, social withdrawal, little or no interest in anything, feelings of inadequacy, reduced effectiveness in school, a pessimistic outlook, an inability to concentrate, and a general "down in the dumps" feeling.

In adolescents, there are occasionally other signs as well. There may be inordinate clinging behavior, usually with peers. It often makes little difference who the other person is (and the other person can change frequently). The behavior involves excessive clinging without real attachment. Depressed adolescents may do anything and everything that the other person asks or may force the other person to do what they want.

There is another specific type of depression, called *agitated depression*, which is characterized by aimless behavior on a regular basis. One gets the feeling that adolescents suffering from this type of depression are ready to explode. There may be twitching or pencil or finger tapping; they may get up to pick up a piece of lint, fumble with papers, or do anything to keep busy. They may leave the house and just walk aimlessly, with no explanation and for no apparent reason. They may drive recklessly, break plans at the very last moment, and then call a friend to do something at eleven o'clock at night. They may go out with friends and then insist on being brought back home after an hour—again with little or no explanation and for no apparent reason.

If your adolescent has enough such symptoms to cause concern and if they persist for several months or more, consider getting help. If you are unsure and don't want to over-react, talk to the school counselor, psychologist, or social worker. These people can help you get some perspective on the situation and can suggest what steps to take next.

RUNNING AWAY

There are different types of runaways and therefore different approaches to the problem. We are not talking about the fifth grader who runs away to the next block with a dozen cookies and three peanut-butter-and-jelly sandwiches, but rather about the runaway who is of high school age, which is a more serious problem.

"I'll Get My Way, Or Else I'll Run Away."

Many teenage runaways come pretty close to having an attitude like this. They are more like the grade school runaway, but they should not be treated the same. They most frequently "run away" to a friend's house to whip their parents into shape: "Do what I say, or I will embarrass you at school and in the community by running away." Sad to say, many parents are bullied by this tactic. One teenage girl explained it this way:

Counselor: Julie, what do you think you will gain by running away?

Julie: After my brother didn't come home for a couple of days, my parents let him stay out as long as he wanted. That's not bad for a couple of days. I can't stand coming in at eleven. I'll give them a few more weeks, and if they haven't changed, I'm taking off.

If this is the situation at your house, the chances are that running away is just one of many problems. It is quite possible that professional help is needed so that you can regain your parenting status. However, there are a few things that you can do right now.

If your adolescent threatens to run away if you don't buy something or allow something *unreasonable*, take the threat very seriously and be very calm and firm. For example, you can say:

> "I can't stop you from running away. However, I want you to know what the consequences will be. If you do run away, you will not be allowed to return to this house until you have agreed to certain conditions. When you return, the following will happen: First, instead of coming in at eleven, you will have to be in the house each night at ten for the next two months. Second, instead of being allowed to go out any night you choose, you will be allowed out only three nights a week for two months. We sincerely hope you will reconsider your decision because we don't really want to make it harder for you, but if you don't reconsider, it is only fair that you know exactly what will happen."

Warning! Do not ever threaten to do anything that you might not do! Decide only on consequences that you are sure you will follow through on. Remember that you will become frightened if your child is missing for a day. Will this make you change your mind? If it will, do not threaten to do what you won't be able to do.

Also be sure that you do not confuse this type of runaway with a much more serious type (discussed next). If you are unclear about what type of potential runaway you have, seek help for your individual situation. Ask people outside the family who know your child. How you handle the situation is still your decision, but additional, third-party information can be very helpful.

The "I Just Can't Take It Anymore" Runaway

The other type of runaway presents a very serious problem and needs a very different approach. A teenager who sees no way out of innumerable problems may run away. The problems may be at home, at school, or with friends, but they are very serious. (The estimate is that more than 50 percent of runaways of this type have been abused, physically or sexually.) These adolescents may have tried many other ways of alerting their parents, but nothing has worked. So now they run away in an attempt to make a desperate call for help, as well as to survive. They usually do not stay in the immediate area. They really run, taking a bus, train, or plane—anything that will enable them to get way.

---

*Getting tough, if and when such a teenager returns, will only make matters worse. Do **not** do it!*

Welcome your son or daughter back and express your concerns. Sit down and talk. Listen carefully and empathetically. Use every ounce of understanding and caring that you can muster. Then matter-of-factly state that you will seek psychological help for your child. For example: "We would appreciate it if you would come with us to a counselor so that we can work this out together." If your child agrees to go—wonderful. If not, go yourself to find out how to help. No book can provide the answers for every individual situation.

DRUG AND ALCOHOL ABUSE

Chapter 3 discussed adolescents' use of drugs and alcohol, which is a common, if frequently disturbing, phenomenon. Occasional use can be handled in the home. Constant use requires outside intervention—therapy or counseling, support groups, and occasionally residential treatment for detoxification and reorientation. But how are parents to distinguish between occasional use and drug or alcohol addiction?

What are the signs? I don't want to get into red eyes, dilated pupils, and so forth, for a number of reasons. First, these physical signs are not reliable. More important, parents who begin examining their teenagers' eyes are ridiculed. There are other more important cues that will not destroy your credibility.

Sign 1: Fairly sudden onset of problems with school

Chapter 4 discussed many reasons for failure in school or sharply reduced performance. In some cases, drug or alcohol abuse is the cause of problems with school. A student who is high from morning until night will hardly hear what goes on in class, let alone study. Such a student must also cut classes in order to drink, smoke marijuana, or take other drugs.

Sign 2: Almost total breakdown in communication with parents for no obvious reasons

Chapters 1 to 4 dealt extensively with normal problems in communication. Drug abuse creates much more severe problems. Teenagers who are drug abusers do not respond positively, despite concerted parental efforts. Living with them is similar to living with an older alcoholic, for, of course, the alcoholic is a drug abuser.

Sign 3: Sudden change in friends

Teenagers often change friends. They may have a fight with one group of friends and move on to another. But usually these changes involve individual friends, not types of friends. If your teenager's friends are good students, the new friends will also be good students. If he or she hangs around with immature, loud kids, the new friends will be immature and loud.

However, if your teenager has had a group of friends whom you were proud to invite to a family picnic and then suddenly begins associating with kids whose vocabulary hardly extends beyond "Hey, man!" and who make Attila the Hun look like Sir Galahad, he or she has made the sudden change in friends referred to here. This can be a sign of drug or alcohol abuse.

Sign 4: Severe mood swings

Joe calls, and Carol is on top of the world. Then Sally calls to tell her that Joe really likes Dara instead, and Carol mopes for two days. That is a normal mood swing. But if Carol is bright, bouncy, and helpful one day, and the next day she swears at you, refuses to do the dishes, and won't come out of her room for dinner, this is a severe mood swing. Too many severe mood swings are another sign of drug or alcohol abuse.

Sign 5: Changes in eating and sleeping habits

A teenager who suddenly decides that staying up all night is cool or who goes from raiding the refrigerator every hour to barely eating anything may also be showing signs of drug or alcohol abuse.

Bright, alert early risers may suddenly start sleeping half the day and getting up tired. Insomnia and sleeping too much are also signs of depression, as is loss of appetite. But they can also point to drug or alcohol abuse. Of course, in most cases, drug and alcohol abusers are also very depressed.

Sign 6: Other changes in behavior

Some people are normally a little paranoid and/or secretive. But if this isn't true of your adolescent, the onset of such behavior is another sign. An adolescent who is neat and conscientious about his or her appearance may become slovenly. An energetic, involved young adult may become morose and lethargic. An adolescent who is interested in theater, sports, or music may suddenly lose all interest for no apparent reason.

Each of the signs discussed above can indicate other problems— serious ones or very normal ones. However, if your teenager shows a number of these signs, the chances of drug or alcohol abuse are good. If you suspect a problem, you should ask school administrators and teachers directly whether your child is part of the drug culture at school or ever appears high or stoned in class.

Teachers are frequently aware of drug or alcohol use or at least suspect it, but do not have sufficient evidence to tell the parents. It is very risky, and even ethically questionable, to accuse a student of drinking or taking drugs without real evidence. If parents ask questions, the matter is easier to discuss.

If your son or daughter does have a drug or alcohol problem, seek professional psychological help at school or ask school officials for the names of the therapists in the community who are most successful with this problem. You might also call a hospital that has an alcoholism and drug detoxification center. The hospital should be able to provide the names of people who can help you.

Placement in a residential facility for detoxification (kicking the habit) is not usually necessary; however, therapy will be ineffective until the drug habit is controlled. A competent therapist with experience in this area can advise you on which course to follow.

TOTALLY OUT-OF-CONTROL TEENAGERS

Adolescents who are totally out of control do what they want when they want. There is no semblance of a parent-child relationship. They may be verbally abusive and occasionally physically abusive. They may steal, lie, run off with the family car without permission, or get drunk or high frequently.

This is not occasional behavior; this is consistent, day-in, day-out, tail-wagging-the-dog behavior. Parents who are faced with this problem may have already tried therapy many times without success. It is impossible for them to determine why the help did not work as well as they had hoped, but it is imperative that they not give up. If you have this problem, seek out a therapist who is strong and will probably make you mad but who will help you do what you have to do to regain control. Be very aware, however, that no therapist alive can help you unless you decide to do something. And what you have to do will be difficult! Unless you are prepared to work harder than you ever have, nothing will change. This is no easy matter.

Unfortunately, most parents of such teenagers are so discouraged that they won't do anything: "We have tried everything; there is nothing anyone can do." This is admittedly a very difficult situation, but please don't give up. Search for a therapist who has had success with such adolescents.

You might also contact an organization called Tough Love, which is a support and information group for parents with out-of-control kids. The address and phone number are given in Chapter 6.

SUICIDE THREATS AND ATTEMPTS

Suicide threats and attempts should *always* be taken seriously. It is true that many are manipulative in nature, but if the situation is so out of hand that an adolescent threatens or attempts suicide, parents should seek professional help for themselves and their child immediately. Such a situation definitely calls for more than self-help. Chapter 6 discusses the details of choosing a therapist.

Warning Signs

1. Most individuals who are thinking of committing suicide actually talk about it. If your child's friends tell you about such threats, thank them and then simply ask your son or daughter, "Have you ever thought about suicide?" Contrary to popular belief, asking about this sympathetically is not harmful. It will not put ideas into a person's head, as some fear. Those who have thought of suicide are frequently relieved to have an opportunity to talk about it.
2. If a usually morose, depressed teenager suddenly becomes cheerful, peaceful, and even euphoric, it is possible that the decision to end it all has brought the momentary peace.
3. Teenagers who are thinking about suicide may get their affairs in order, such as by giving a favorite record to a sister they are always fighting with or by giving other valuable possessions to friends.

If you have any reason to suspect that your teenager is thinking of suicide, ask. If the response is positive or hesitant, seek help immediately! It is also important to realize that many people think about suicide but that only a few actually plan it. It is possible that your teenager is not in serious danger if he or she has only thought about it. But a successful suicide attempt doesn't leave anyone a second chance. So let someone else who is highly trained judge the extent of the danger. The problem is too serious for parents to try to handle it themselves.

Chapter 6

Where and How To Get Help

There are many different types of mental health specialists as well as myriad approaches and techniques. The cost can range from nothing to over $100 an hour. In addition to specialists, there are self-help and support groups. How can parents know where to turn when psychological help is needed? This chapter provides step-by-step guidelines as well as the information needed to make an informed decision.

Mental health specialists are differentiated according to formal training and/or degrees earned—psychologist, psychiatrist, etc. However, one general term is used to refer to these people—*therapist* or *psychotherapist*. He or she has been trained to help people understand themselves and others better; to help individuals, families, or groups change troublesome behaviors; and to teach new behaviors that will help people lead fuller, happier lives. No one can make you or your child better. The specialist can only facilitate the process. The client has to work, and work hard, for there to be any meaningful progress.

MENTAL HEALTH SPECIALISTS

Psychologists

In most states, only individuals with a Ph.D. or a Psy.D. in psychology or counseling can refer to themselves as psychologists. A person who has a Ph.D. in psychology has not necessarily been trained as a therapist. There are industrial psychologists, social psychologists, psychologists who specialize in tests and measurements, etc. The professional you should seek out for therapeutic services is called a *clinical psychologist*. Ask the individual whether he or she has served as a clinical intern or has completed a supervised therapy practicum. A person with a Psy.D. is always a clinical psychologist.

Psychologists can espouse any school of thought (see the discussion of types of therapy later in this chapter). This is the area of greatest diversification in the mental health field. Psychologists have been at the forefront of new and better approaches to a wide range of problems.

In most states, a psychologist who is licensed can sign insurance forms. Those in private practice normally charge from $50 to $90 an hour. Those who cannot sign insurance forms charge considerably less, sometimes half as much as licensed psychologists or psychiatrists.

School Psychologists

These professionals have at least a master's degree in psychology. Many are trained therapists. Their particular approach depends on their training and their personal preference.

When they work for the school, their services to you and your child are free. However, they are less flexible in terms of time than individuals in private practice. Usually the school psychologist is available only during the hours that the school is open. Many schools do not have a sufficient number of therapists to serve students who need therapy. If your child attends such a school, your only choice is to seek outside help.

Social Workers

Social workers have a master's degree in social work. Social workers are always trained as therapists, and they work in many settings—schools, hospitals, agencies, and private practice. Most high schools have a social worker whose therapeutic services are free. In most states social workers cannot sign insurance forms, so those who are in private practice usually charge considerably less than licensed psychologists or psychiatrists.

School Counselors

These people have at least a master's degree and have been trained in counseling skills. However, not all counselors have the time or training required to provide therapy. When in doubt, ask.

Counselors

The term *counselor* is used to describe 14-year-old kids who oversee 8-year-olds at camp. It is used by lawyers, bankers, brokers, and travel agents—you name it! It is not a legally protected term, like *psychologist*. In some states, for instance, anyone can call himself or herself a marriage counselor, regardless of training. All you need to do is check on where the counselor you are considering received his or her training and whether he or she has provided therapy under supervision.

Psychiatrists

Psychiatrists are medical doctors who specialize in psychiatry instead of internal medicine or gynecology, for example. They are the only ones who can prescribe medication. They tend to deal with people who have more serious, chronic mental illnesses and who require occasional hospitalization and almost constant medication to maintain even a modicum of normal functioning. While many psychiatrists are trained as therapists, a large number choose to focus on the biochemical aspects of behavior. They may speak with patients about what's bothering them in much the same way that an understanding general practitioner does. But the "therapy," the means for helping the person function or function better, is medication. There are many drugs that work wonders. The competent psychiatrist prescribes the right drugs in the right dosage to help the person function.

Drugs do not cure mental illness; they simply make it possible for some people to act in a more normal way, or they alleviate the debilitating feelings of depression. Some individuals want only this. They are not interested in learning new behaviors or in changing in any other way. They just don't want to suffer as much, or their relatives cannot take care of them when they "act crazy."

The costs of the services of a psychiatrist can differ a great deal, but $70 to $100 an hour (an "hour" usually lasts from forty-five to fifty minutes) is not uncommon, and some may charge more than this in certain circumstances.

Health insurance can cover all or part of this expense. Most policies, however, have restrictions, such as 50 percent payment and/or a certain time limit on treatment. Check yours carefully before considering its use.

TYPES OF THERAPY

The type of therapy is not as important as the skill of the therapist. All schools and approaches are effective if the therapist is good and the patient, or client, wants to change. Both components are necessary. Following is a brief description of the major types of therapy. This is not essential knowledge for choosing a therapist. It is included here for those who are curious and want the information. Please remember, however, that it is more important to search for a good therapist than a "good" school of thought.

Psychoanalysis

Psychoanalysis is based on Freud's basic concepts. One of its major assumptions about the human personality is that thoughts, feelings, and actions are determined by events in the person's past.

Psychoanalysis is considerably different from the other approaches. This is the only approach in which the patient lies on a couch during therapy, although most people who have not been to a therapist believe that lying on a couch is common practice.

Once on the couch, the patient is asked to tell the therapist whatever thoughts, images, and feelings come to mind. Occasionally the analyst (therapist) interrupts this free flow of words to make connections between various items.

Psychoanalysis requires a tremendous investment of time (possibly several sessions a week for several years) and money, and it is essential that the patient be highly motivated to overcome whatever difficulties he or she is experiencing. It is not the recommended treatment for most adolescents.

The Freudian Approach

This is a loose, nonscientific term. The Freudian approach is used by therapists with many different orientations—ego psychologists, object relationists, etc.—and is based on Freud's personality theories and basic psychological concepts. The therapist talks about the conscious and the unconscious, drives, defense mechanisms, and the like. These terms have become part of everyday language, but they have specific meanings and applications in a Freudian approach to psychotherapy.

This approach differs from psychoanalysis in a number of important ways. The client sits in a chair rather than lying on a couch. Free association may be used occasionally, but it is not the primary therapeutic mode. Therapy is usually a long-term procedure. The therapist encourages the client to discuss the past in an attempt to find the cause or causes of the current behavior or feelings. The therapist is also likely to see an individual once a week rather than three or four times a week.

Adlerian Psychotherapy

Adler was a contemporary of Freud who eventually disagreed with him on most major points. Adler, for instance, believed that we are goal-directed—that behavior is not determined by past events and that we are free and very responsible for our thoughts, feelings, and actions.

Adlerian therapists examine clients' lifestyles or ways of approaching life and try to help them become aware of what they are doing and decide whether they want to continue their current behavior. If an individual wants to change, therapy is a cooperative educational enterprise. The therapist is more interested in strengths that the individual can build on than in weaknesses that must be changed.

Many people have been introduced to Adlerian ideas in study groups or in books by Rudolf Dreikurs (*Children the Challenge* is one of his most popular). Adler and many who have followed him are more interested in preventing problems than in "fixing them up" after they develop. Hence, there is a strong emphasis on working with normal children and families to help prevent bigger problems from arising later.

Adlerian therapy is very practical, especially for families. There is more emphasis on problem solving than on probing the psyche.

Person-Centered, or Client-Centered, Therapy

This therapeutic approach was developed by Carl Rogers in the 1940s. Its central idea is that clients will grow and become better if they are in a relationship with a therapist who is caring, deeply sensitive, and totally nonjudgmental. The therapist's ability to really care for the client and really listen is crucial. In addition, the therapist has been trained to reflect certain statements or feelings in such a way that the client can learn and grow. The therapist gives little or no advice or direction. The belief is that, given the proper conditions, clients will discover the best way to proceed by themselves.

Therapy does not involve understanding the past or even talking about it. The present experiences of the client are the focus of the therapy.

Rational-Emotive Therapy (RET)

RET was developed by Albert Ellis in the 1950s. Whereas a person-centered therapist is very "laid back" and nondirective, a rational-emotive therapist is very active, even aggressive, in helping clients see the irrationality of some of their beliefs. The theory is that beliefs or thoughts cause emotions; therefore, if irrational thoughts are diligently disputed and challenged, undesirable emotional consequences (such as severe anxiety) will eventually disappear.

Rational-emotive therapists do not believe that a warm relationship between therapist and client is necessary for change to occur. Clients are accepted, but they may also be criticized for some of their behavior. Other therapy techniques include behavior modification, homework (or behavior to practice before the next session), and role playing.

Compared with other current, respected therapeutic approaches, person-centered therapy involves the most warmth and the fewest directive statements. RET, which is confrontational and directive, is at the other end of the spectrum. Adlerian therapy is somewhere in the middle.

Behavioral Psychotherapy

Behavioral psychotherapy stems from the work of Joseph Wolpe, B. F. Skinner, and others. Emotional pain is believed to be the result of ineffective or maladaptive learning. Therefore, the purpose of psychotherapy is to help the client relearn some behaviors and learn others that are new. In that respect, it is similar to RET. There is a strong emphasis on practice, homework, and practical techniques for effecting behavior change, as well as on establishing a working relationship with the client.

Therapists who espouse other schools of thought also use some of the active, change-producing techniques employed by behaviorists. Relaxation training and assertiveness training are popular and are very useful in a number of situations.

Gestalt Therapy

This school of thought was founded by Fritz Perls (1893–1970). It is another modern therapeutic approach which emphasizes personal, here-and-now responsibility rather than delving into the past to discover the causes of current behavior.

One of the major differences between gestalt therapy and other therapies, however, is its emphasis on biological functions. Perls believed that every human activity should be regarded as a biological process. Gestalt therapy emphasizes being in touch with the biological self—with the physiological components of one's thoughts and emotions.

The therapy involves knowing all the parts of the self (the processes of the self); examining them, or "chewing on" them; and then either accepting and assimilating what is palatable or rejecting what is distasteful. The process involves a striving for authenticity.

Reality Therapy

Developed by William Glasser in the 1950s, reality therapy assumes that personal responsibility for one's own behavior can be equated with mental health. In reality therapy, the client is helped to clarify and define both long-term and short-term goals. As in the Adlerian model, therapy is an educational process—a learning process rather than a "getting well." The focus is always on the present rather than the past.

Transactional Analysis (TA)

TA, as it is popularly called, originated with Eric Berne in the 1950s. His best-seller, *Games People Play*, popularized the theory.

Unlike most other modern therapeutic approaches, Berne's personality theory divides the person into battling ego states: the Parent, the Adult, and the Child. Many find it difficult to see how these are very different from Freud's superego, ego, and id. However, Berne does differ from Freud in some important ways. First, he doesn't attach nearly as much importance to the unconscious, and second, the therapist is more active and involved than in psychoanalytic approaches.

Family Therapy

Family Therapy is a confusing term since it can encompass both a specific approach to therapy (Adlerian, for example) and a type of therapy (such as individual, group, or family). Most therapeutic systems can be used with an individual, with a couple seeking marriage counseling, with groups of nonrelated individuals, or with a family.

The beginnings of family therapy as a specific approach are unclear, and many have contributed to its development. In this therapy, the family is the client—not an individual in the family who is experiencing problems or causing the problems for other family members. The purpose of the therapy is not to help the troublesome individual change but rather to change the relationships between the family members so that the undesirable behavior or symptoms will disappear. The theory is that the problem is not with the individual but with the family system and that if you change the system, you will change the individual.

Eclectic Approaches

Eclectic means "composed from various systems, doctrines, or sources." If a person says that he or she uses an eclectic approach to psychotherapy, this means that the individual picks and chooses from among many different schools of thought, using what makes sense or what works.

Although some therapists who use an eclectic approach are very experienced and have worked out a highly sophisticated individual system, others are inexperienced and have no real training in any approach.

Summary

The above is a deliberately brief overview of the major therapeutic approaches currently in use. It is presented so that you will have some knowledge of what therapy is available. But as was noted above, the type of therapy is not as important as the individual therapist. So although it is nice to know a little about the various schools of thought, it is much more important to find a good therapist whom you like and feel comfortable with.

HOW TO FIND A GOOD THERAPIST

It is possible to receive excellent therapy free by utilizing the services of the school psychologist, social worker, or counselor, if he or she has the time. If you would rather seek help outside the school system, these three people are good referral sources. They frequently know people in the area who are especially good with teenagers. This is very important. For example, although Dr. X treated Aunt Sophie's depression superbly, there is little guarantee that he has had experience dealing with teenagers. In fact, the chances are good that Dr. X will try to treat an adolescent as he would treat an adult, and this approach will not work.

If you wish to remain anonymous when seeking a referral, just call the school, describe your situation briefly, and ask for recommendations. A pediatrician might also know someone who works well with teenagers.

If relatives, friends, or neighbors have had problems with their teenagers, you might ask whether they can recommend someone. Church leaders can also steer you toward good therapists in the community.

You can also contact the organizations listed below for the names of therapists in your area. The addresses and phone numbers given are those of the national offices. In many large cities there are local offices, especially of the American Psychological Association.

American Psychological Association
Office of Professional Affairs
1200 17th St. N.W.
Washington, D.C. 20036
(202)833-7600

The Association for Advancement of
Behavior Therapy
420 Lexington Ave.
New York, N.Y. 10170
(212)682-0065

The National Mental Health Association
1800 N. Kent St.
Arlington, Va. 22036
(703)528-6405

American Psychiatric Association
1700 18th St. N.W.
Washington, D.C. 20009

The fact is, however, that no matter how carefully you select a therapist, there are no guarantees. A therapist who has

helped innumerable teenagers and their families may be ineffective with your adolescent and your family. If either you or
your teenager is dissatisfied, don't give up. Seek out someone
else. If the problems are so serious that you need help, continue searching.

FEAR OF THERAPY AND OF CHANGE

There are times, however, when no one will make an impact
and when nothing you do will seem to help. If you or your
adolescent refuses to change, no one can force either of you to
do so. The results of deciding not to change may be disastrous,
but each of us can make such a decision. It is important to
realize that you have a choice. For example:

"I'm too old to change."

"How do you expect someone as sick as me to change?"

"I just can't help it; it's the way I am."

"If I change, then she wins. No way."

These are all *choices*. No one is a hapless victim. Our excuses
may sound different, but they all come down to the very same
thing: *"I will not change!"*

One of the biggest problems with therapy for adolescents
and their families is the tendency to make going to therapy
itself part of the fight. An illustration might help:

Alice   No way I'm going to a shrink. My parents think
(age 17): they're so perfect. They've really got their nerve
          thinking they're going to fix me up, as if it's my
          fault or something. My mother is crazier than a
          loon, and my father isn't far behind, but they
          want to send *me* to a shrink. I'd like to see them
          try!

Alice's parents respond this way:

Mother: Of course we won't go with her. She's the one
          who is crazy—all the things she's pulled. We're
          sure she's on something, too.

Father: We'll be happy to pay someone to straighten her out, but I've got to support my family. I'm not wasting an hour a week talking to someone when it's Alice's problem. Anyhow, I don't believe in all that stuff. I think they're crazier than the people they work with anyway. How could talking ever help this mess? Let Alice go; I'm not going.

This family still believes that only "crazy" people go for psychological help. Nothing could be further from the truth. Most individuals or families in therapy are there to improve their lives; they are not crazy. Most people who go to medical doctors are not dying. They may have the flu, a broken thumb, or a backache. So it is with psychological help. It is tragic to avoid therapy when intervention can help so much.

Fear of change, fear of revealing too much, anger at parents or at children, and not knowing what will happen—these are all understandable reasons for reluctance. But none is sufficient reason for doing nothing.

It isn't just Alice's problem. If Alice is seriously acting out and the family is at war, this is a problem for the *entire family.* Usually if parents approach the situation with cooperation and understanding, the teenager will be able to relax a little and do his or her share. For instance, Alice's mother might say:

> "Alice, something is definitely wrong here, and we feel a real need to work something out. We have tried everything else without success, so your father and I are going to a counselor. We would appreciate it if you would come with us. Why don't you think about it and let us know?"

Alice may not go right away, but after she sees her parents going for a while, she will probably join them. She will want to get her side of the story in too.

Realize that your teenager's problem is also your problem. If your daughter is stealing the local stores blind, has failed most of her classes at school, or comes home high most nights of the week, you have a problem. You are not responsible for her behavior, but you still have a problem. If she won't go for counseling with you, at least you can go to learn how to deal with the situation better. You can be responsible only for what you do and for the decisions you make. It is impossible to force your teenager to change. But without a doubt, the changes you make in your own behavior will have a powerful effect on your adolescent.

PAYING FOR THERAPY

How much you pay for therapy depends on how much you make as well as on how much you are willing to sacrifice to get help. Some parents have told me that they can't afford therapy, but the following week they spend $12,000 for a new car or take a vacation in Hawaii. Like anything else, it's a matter of priorities, not just income. "But I don't even know if it will help," some have retorted. No one knows whether a new car is a lemon or whether it will rain for twelve out of thirteen vacation days either. There are no guarantees for anything. So the first thing is to put the problem in perspective. How much is therapy worth to you? How many sacrifices are you willing to make? Your answer may be "very few." All right, that is honest. Don't hide behind excuses. There are no excuses for not getting help when it is necessary.

It also does not follow that the most expensive therapist is the best. It is not always true that you get what you pay for. Quality—not cost—is the issue. But if money is an important factor, you might try the following options:

- *Free Therapy*: The school psychologist, social worker, or counselor may have the time to offer free therapy. Many schools do not hire enough mental health specialists to allow these people to provide therapeutic services. Their days are filled with other tasks mandated by special education laws or district policy.
- *Sliding-Scale Plans*: Therapy offered on a sliding-scale basis can range from free to approximately $40 an hour or

more, based on family income. Public agencies and some private ones will provide therapy at a cost the family can afford. You can find the public agencies in your area by looking under Social Service Organizations in the yellow pages. You may find others listed under Mental Health Services or Mental Health Clinics. (Some of those listed in the yellow pages do not charge on a sliding scale. Call to check.) You can also call the school, church leaders, the local hospital, or the youth officer at the police station. There are some private, nonprofit agencies which also charge on a sliding-scale basis. The Salvation Army Mental Health Centers, Catholic Charities, and Jewish Family Services are examples.

Training schools for psychiatrists, psychologists, social workers, and mental health counselors also provide inexpensive service. The therapists are in training, but they are closely supervised by some of the best people in the mental health field. The fact that they are in training does not mean that they are inexperienced. Many have returned to school to learn new methods or sharpen their skills after years of working as therapists.

Obtaining help at most agencies is a little different from calling for an appointment with a private practitioner. When you go in for the first appointment, you will probably talk to an intake worker. This person will ask for information about you and about what you would like to gain from therapy. After this initial interview, you will be assigned to a therapist who can best work with you.

The therapists at public and private agencies can be psychologists with a master's degree, social workers, or counselors. There is usually one or more Ph.D. or Psy.D. psychologists on the staff for consultation and perhaps a psychiatrist who advises on medication or hospitalization when necessary.

$25 to $50 an Hour: Therapists in private practice who do not sign insurance forms charge in this range.

$40 to $90 an Hour or More: Therapists who can sign insur-

ance forms charge in this range. These are usually doctoral-level psychologists and psychiatrists.

GROUPS TO CONTACT

In addition to seeking therapeutic intervention, you can also contact a number of groups that can provide information, support, and hope. These groups have been nothing short of salvation for innumerable individuals and their families. Others have found them mildly helpful to not helpful at all. It is impossible to predict the outcome for you, but it is certainly worthwhile to obtain information about such groups and perhaps go to a meeting or two.

Alcoholism

The Johnson Institute
10700 Olson Memorial Highway
Minneapolis, Minn. 55441

The Johnson Institute originated the intervention approach to alcoholism. This is an effective, family-involved approach that requires a trained counselor on a fairly short-term basis. Write the Johnson Institute for the names of trained counselors in your area.

Alcoholics Anonymous (AA)
Box 459
Grand Central Station
New York, N.Y. 10163

You can also check your telephone directory for a local number and/or address. Information on local groups will be sent in a plain envelope.

Al Anon Family Groups
Box 182
Madison Square Station
New York, N.Y. 10159

Al Anon provides support, encouragement, and information for persons close to alcoholics.

Alateen

This is a subgroup of Al Anon for teenage children of alcoholics.

The National Clearinghouse for
Alcohol Information
Box 2345
Rockville, Md. 20852

This organization offers literature on all aspects of alcoholism. It also has local lists of public and private counseling and treatment facilities. Request a plain envelope if you prefer.

National Council on Alcoholism
733 Third Ave.
New York, N.Y. 10017

The National Council on Alcoholism can provide a list of organizations in various cities that can refer clients to public and private treatment agencies.

Anorexia Nervosa and Bulimia

Anorexia Nervosa and
Associated Eating Disorders
Suite 2020
550 Frontage Rd.
Northfield, Ill. 60093
(312)831-3438

or

Box 271
Highland Park, Ill. 60035

This organization is made up of people who are concerned with anorexia nervosa, bulimia, and other eating disorders. Call or write for information on self-help groups, the names of recommended therapists and physicians, and general information.

Cancer

Candlelighters
123 C St., S.E.
Washington, D.C. 20003

This organization provides information about self-help groups for parents of cancer victims.

Child Abuse

National Center on Child Abuse and Neglect
400 6th Ave.
Washington, D.C. 20201
(202)245-2859

Parents Anonymous
2810 Artesia Blvd.
Suite F
Redondo Beach, Calif. 90278
(800)421-0353
(800)352-0386 (California)

This organization offers a free self-help program for parents who want to stop abusing their children. (To report a case of child abuse, call the local police station or a local hotline number for this purpose.)

Death of a Child

Compassionate Friends
Box 1314
Oak Brook, Ill. 60521

The purpose of this group is to offer support and understanding to parents who have lost a child. There are local groups across the country.

Drug Abuse

Drug Abuse Council
1828 L St., N.W.
Washington, D.C. 20036

Families Anonymous
Box 344
Torrance, Calif. 90501

This organization offers help to parents of children who are addicted to drugs.

Narconon
3636 Grand Ave. S., 303
Minneapolis, Minn. 55409

Narconon can provide information on rehabilitation of drug addicts.

National Clearinghouse for Drug Abuse Information
5600 Fishers La.
Rockville, Md. 20852

Homosexuality

Dignity
755 Boylston Ave.
Room 413
Boston, Mass. 02116

Parents of Gays
201 West 13th St.
New York, N.Y. 10011

or

Box 24528
Los Angeles, Calif. 90024

Out-of-Control Teenagers

Tough Love
Community Service Foundation
Box 70
Sellersville, Pa. 18960
(215)766-8022

The basic premise of this organization is that no parent need accept or feel guilty about out-of-control adolescents. Literature, self-help groups, and workshops are geared at teaching parents "tough love"—how to regain control. This organization should not be an alternative to therapy. It's a support group.

Rape

Check the phone book for local organizations that help rape victims or call the emergency room of your local hospital. You may also contact:

Family Service Association
44 East 23d St.
New York, N.Y. 10010

Runaways

National Runaway Hotline
(800)621-4000
(800)972-6004 (Illinois)

This hotline provides free advisory services to runaways and their parents, twenty-four hours a day, on a confidential basis.

Operation Peace of Mind
(800)231-6946
(800)392-3352 (Texas)

This is a confidential, twenty-four-hour-a day message relay service established to accept calls from runaways and forward messages to parents. This organization provides counseling and confidential referral information on medical assistance, shelter, and other counseling services.

Suicide Prevention

Crisis Intervention and Suicide Prevention Program
4200 N. Oak Park Ave.
Chicago, Ill. 60634
(312)794-3609

Venereal Disease (VD)

VD Hotline
(800)462-4966 (Pennsylvania)
(800)523-1885

This hotline provides confidential, anonymous, free consultation, information, and referral services on all aspects of sexually transmitted diseases.

Chapter 7

Single Parents and Stepparents

Approximately one-third of today's high school students do not live with both parents. This is no longer an unusual situation. However, one-parent families and homes in which there is a stepparent do have special problems not common in other households.

ONE-PARENT FAMILIES: DIVORCED PARENTS

Divorced parents can have a number of harmful reactions and responses to the breakup of a marriage:

1. Feeling guilty
2. Crying on their children's shoulders—the "rotten-rat" syndrome
3. Threatening to send the children to the other parent—the "shape up or get out" tactic
4. Making excuses for the former spouse
5. Blaming the children for the divorce

Guilt

Guilt is unfortunately still a big problem. One or both parents feel guilty about the supposed harm done to the children. Divorced parents should not feel guilty. Feeling guilty is the best way in the world to make a separation or divorce a bad thing for kids. Following are some of the consequences of feeling guilty.

"I have to make it up to them."

Mom has finally divorced a brutal husband, but she feels guilty for having subjected her children to his brutality for so many years. Now she tries to make up for all the pain they suffered. She buys them things she can't afford, and she lets them get away with murder in the hope that they will not hate her for putting them through such a terrible childhood. Parents in this situation should remember the following:

- A mother is *not* responsible for what the father did or did not do. Only the father can be responsible for that.
- There is no way to make up for lost time, affection, or anything else. All that is possible is to do a good parenting job today. That is difficult enough in itself without trying to make up for actual or supposed injustices in the past.
- Trying to fix things up by overcompensating almost always leads to inappropriate parenting. Teenagers can sense guilt, and unfortunately many of them use it to get what they want. If extravagant gifts were inappropriate before the divorce, they are inappropriate now. If coming in at 2 A.M. was unacceptable before the divorce, it is unacceptable now.

Here is another example of overcompensating. Mom has the children, but she feels responsible for the breakup. She can't live with the children's father, but she sees him as a good father and feels guilty that she has virtually taken the kids away from him. She also tries hard to be extra nice to the kids, so they pour the guilt on even more:

"Gee, I sure miss Dad."

"I'd feel a lot better if we could see Dad more often."

Taken in themselves, these are legitimate, feeling statements that should receive responses like:

"It hurts when we can't see someone we love as often as we would like."

"I'm sorry you feel sad."

But to take such statements as signals to feel guilty is destructive. It is normal for children to miss their father. It is not good for their mother to feel guilty because, as the first example shows, guilt can frequently lead to inappropriate parenting.

"It's all my fault."

Father gets the children on weekends. He feels guilty about the breakup, and the kids know it. They do a very common thing: they plot and plan to get their parents back together. They say things like:

"Dad, why don't you just apologize and come back home?"

"Mom really misses you."

"It's just not the same without you at home."

"I've been doing poorly in school since you left."

Of course it's hard on children when parents break up. It's very hard on the parents too. That's expected, but it need not be devastating. It is a part of life. Life can sometimes be hard. There is no way to shield kids from all pain.

It is always hard to see your own children suffer. It is even harder when you feel responsible for the pain. But it is not a reason to feel guilty. You can love them, comfort them, and play with them, but you can't wave a magic wand that will take the pain away. You can only be a good parent today. No one can ask for more.

Guilt is bad for you, and it's bad for your children. If you can't get rid of it on your own in a reasonable amount of time, seek some counseling to help you through this difficult period.

The Rotten-Rat Syndrome

The rotten-rat syndrome is hard to avoid in a particularly messy or bitter divorce. Sometimes the anger and hostility toward a former mate can almost consume you. You need comfort and understanding very badly. It is hard not to cry on your teenagers' shoulders—to get them to agree with your own assessment of what went wrong and with your own assessment of what a rotten rat your former spouse is.

Parents who are caught in this trap know that demeaning a former spouse in front of the children is not good. But since it is so hard to avoid, some parents justify it by saying, for example:

"I want to be sure my kids aren't hurt the way I was. I have to warn them."

"They can't stand her either. I'm not saying anything they don't already feel."

Occasionally children will bad-mouth one of the parents simply because kids get mad at parents all the time. It's normal. But it isn't normal for a child to hate a parent. When children are made to feel that they must hate one parent to show the other loyalty, serious problems can develop.

If a child goes through a period of genuinely despising a parent, it is not appropriate for the other parent to encourage or help increase the feeling. After a certain time your adolescent will want to establish better ties with the other parent, and if you have encouraged hate, these ties will seem like treason toward you. That will complicate an already difficult situation.

"Why shouldn't I tell the kids what he's like? It's the truth, isn't it?" It may be objectively, verifiably true that a former spouse is as bad as you believe, but most young children and adolescents cannot handle that fact. This is definitely one situation in which telling the truth has a very negative effect. It hurts your kids too much to justify doing it. They aren't blind or stupid; they know their parents' faults and transgressions only too well. But they frequently can't handle being told about them all the time.

"If You Don't Shape Up. . . ."

"If you don't shape up, you can go live with your father." Threatening to send a teenager to live with the other parent is a two-edged, very sharp sword that must be used with extreme care. Having this option can be a blessing, but it can also lead to problems.

Making such a threat is worse than saying, "If you don't shape up, I'll kick you out of the house." It's worse because it is definitely more possible. As a rule, such threats make teenagers feel rejected and very insecure. Frequently, acting-out behavior will increase rather than decrease. This behavior can be an angry retaliation, or it can be an attempt to push the parent into carrying out the threat. Some adolescents would rather be sent immediately to the other parent—even if they hate the idea—than live on pins and needles worrying about it. At least if they go now, it will be over and they can try to rebuild their lives.

Nonetheless, there are times when it is in everyone's best interests to send a teenager to live with the other parent. It is possible that (1) the other parent may handle teenagers better or (2) the adolescent's behavior is out of control, and a new approach is required. It is important, however, to distinguish between normal, aggravating adolescent behavior and real out-of-control behavior. (See Chapters 1 to 5.)

In the case of out-of-control behavior, it is necessary, or certainly advisable, to discuss the issue rationally rather than to make the decision in a moment of fear or anger. Nothing is so bad that it can't wait for things to calm down. In a calm moment, a conversation about living with the other parent might go as follows:

Father: I am becoming very frightened by your behavior. This is the second time in a month I've had to get you at the police station, and you've come home drunk so many times that I've lost count.

Joan: But Dad, I won't do it again.

Father: Joan, I know you don't want to do it again, but let's face facts. You have done it many times after promising "never again." It just can't go on forever. You and I both know that. I love you too much to allow you to ruin your life. Do you think you might be able to work things out better if you went to live with your mother? She has agreed to take you and go for counseling with you.

Joan: Well, I would rather not, but it may be the only way I'll get myself straightened out. I just don't know right now.

This discussion could go on for a long time, but the main point is that the change would be for the purpose of helping Joan, not just her father. Enlisting Joan's ideas and cooperation is much better than sending her off as a kind of punishment. It is possible that her father will eventually have to insist on her going, but it will not be a last-ditch, angry decision. It will have been thought out and talked about beforehand.

As was mentioned above, suggesting that a teenager live with the other parent is a two-edged sword; the other side of the sword cuts this way: "I hate living here; I'm going to go live with Dad. He won't treat me like a stupid child. I should have lived with him from the beginning." This hurts *so* much. You work your head off and do the best you can without any help. The whole responsibility is on you, and you're very tired. You feel as if you're carrying the world on your shoulders, and you've just about had it. And then your smart-aleck kid stands there and has the nerve to say this! The easiest reaction is, "You want to go live with him? Go right ahead. I'll call him right now. Get the hell out of my life. Who needs this?"

That might be the easiest response, but you should try not to make it, if possible. If it comes out anyway, it's not the end of the world, but there are obviously other alternatives that might be better. Knowing why teenagers say such things may help you make the best response in your situation.

Sometimes your child is just plain angry and knows that this comeback will hurt you. That is the purpose—to hurt you.

Other teenagers may be testing the parent or may fear that if they don't go themselves, they will be forced to leave. They would rather make it look as if they want to go so that the parent won't punish them by sending them. That's a little complicated, but it's a self-protective device that is used all the time.

Let us assume that you threaten to punish your son by sending him to his room: "The next time you talk back, I'm sending you to your room all evening." The next day, he may casually comment on how enjoyable it is to spend time in his room. It's so nice and quiet, and he can get so much done. Then if you send him to his room, he wins. It isn't a punishment. After all, he just told you how much he likes it there. He wants to make you feel as if you're punishing him with an ice-cream cone. It makes a joke of the punishment.

Something similar happens when teenagers talk about living with the other parent. If they fear that they will be sent there, they at least want to go in dignity, not in disgrace. It is still a punishment, but they are the only ones who know it.

But what if the situation is so bad that it is necessary to send your son or daughter to live with the other parent? Then be sure the details are clear:

- There will be no moving back at least until the end of the school year. If that is only a few months away, there will be no moving back until the end of the following school year.
- If the child pushed for the move, coming back will not be permitted automatically, upon request. It will be discussed and negotiated. It is important for the child to realize that this is serious. Moving from house to house cannot be used as a club by the parents or the child.

Of course, we are talking here about an actual change of residence and probably of custody. There are less drastic means of bringing about a needed separation. If the father usually takes the children for two weeks in the summer, perhaps one summer he can keep them for two months to give everyone a break from the fighting or whatever else is going on. That's different. Taking longer vacations or having a week's cooling-off period can be a big advantage in two-parent, two-home situations. Such arrangements are very different from forcing teenagers to move or from allowing them to force you to let them move.

Making Excuses for a Former Spouse

Just as it isn't good to drive a former spouse into the ground in front of the children, neither is it necessary or even good to make excuses for that person's behavior. If, for instance, your children's father doesn't call the kids, see them, or even send them gifts on their birthdays or other occasions, it is not necessary for you to make excuses for him: "He is probably very busy," or "You know how forgetful he is." Your kids won't buy this any more than you do, so just drop it. Simply listen and understand. You cannot be two parents. You cannot assume responsibility for the other parent's behavior. A good way to handle this situation is as follows:

Sally: Dad, is it that hard for Mom to remember my birthday? I don't really expect her to buy me anything. If she could just call or even send a card.

Father: It's very disappointing when someone you love forgets your birthday. It hurts.

Sally: Yes, it hurts a lot. Sometimes I think she doesn't even love me anymore.

At this point, it would probably be best for Sally's father just to hug her and let her cry. There really isn't anything he can say. There isn't anything else he *should* say. The problem is between Sally and her mother. Sally should eventually talk to her about it, but this is probably not the time. It certainly isn't the time for her father to suggest it.

Blaming the Children for the Divorce

The trauma of disagreements and fighting that eventually end in divorce can lead to rash, untrue statements that harm the children. It is not unusual for one or both parents to blame the children—especially acting-out teenagers—for the dissolution of the marriage. When the parents are in such turmoil, trying to place the blame elsewhere is understandable but very dangerous. Most children are not harmed by divorce. If any harm results at all, it is usually due to parents' inappropriate reactions to the divorce. Blaming the children is one of the worst.

Children of all ages tend to blame themselves anyway. When parents add to this by actually accusing them, all kinds of havoc can result.

It is important that parents give a clear message to their children: "You are not responsible for our divorce. No matter how it may occasionally appear to you, *you are not responsible*. It is between your father and me."

It is also helpful in this situation to tell children that *they can still love the other parent*. This is always a problem if a child feels that loving one parent is a kind of disloyalty to the other parent. It is especially difficult in the case of adultery or alcoholism, for example, where one parent's behavior is seen as the "cause" of the divorce. No matter what the circumstances, children should not feel that they have to reject a parent. The only way to avoid this is to make it clear in words and actions: "Your mother and I obviously have serious problems, but that doesn't mean that you can't love your mother."

If it is difficult to see your children visit your former spouse or enjoy the visit, it is probably better to address the matter directly. For some, it's a very difficult feeling to hide:

> "You may sense that sometimes I don't like it when you go to visit dad. That's really my problem and not something I want to impose on you. It is good that you go, and it is good that you enjoy the visit. Please be patient with me. It may take a while before I respond the way I'd like to."

STEPPARENTS

Teenagers frequently feel resentment when a parent remarries. It can be very mild or very severe. but it is almost always there. The "why" is sometimes not clear to them or to others, but there are some common explanations.

One reason is that the second marriage ends the daydream of getting the parents together again. Many children of all ages hope for a reconciliation, even when the marriage made the home a war zone. They will verbally acknowledge that such a hope is crazy, but the hope is still there. The remarriage adds a second finality, so to speak. The divorce was not quite enough; the remarriage ends the hope forever.

The new spouse will also take a lot of the parent's time—time the kids were used to spending with the parent. Many teenagers are happy to have more time to themselves, but others resent the time devoted to the new spouse.

If you feel this might be the case with your children, there are a number of ways in which you can deal with the situation without reverting to past patterns. Having breakfast or lunch in a restaurant alone with your children can go a long way toward making them feel special. Another alternative is to spend half an hour or an hour a week alone with each child. Even fifteen minutes can be very helpful. You can sit and talk, go shopping, or go for a walk. What you do isn't as important as the fact that this is the individual child's special time with you.

The strongest feelings against a stepparent—especially among teenagers—have to do with the stepparent's "taking over." A 15-year-old boy put it this way: "He's not a bad guy or anything, but he's a stranger in the house as far as I'm concerned. Who does he think he is, yelling at me and telling me what to do? He isn't my father, and he damn well better get that straight."

This is perhaps the most sensitive, difficult situation that stepparents face. It causes the most frustration and occasionally also the most arguments with the new spouse. In most situations, especially where even one of the children is about 10 or older, it is probably best for the natural parent to do the disciplining. A very sensitive, successful stepparent stated that assuming a role similar to that of a favorite aunt or uncle seems to work best, even when the stepchildren are in the same house. She described it as a "real lesson in self-restraint" for everyone involved, but said that in the long run it avoids many problems.

A parent who has had full responsibility for the children and who remarries has a tendency to "let someone else handle it for a while." This is definitely not recommended. Allow the children—especially older ones—to get used to the idea of a stepparent slowly.

Often the most difficulty is with the oldest child in the family. In a one-parent family, an older child can take on a lot of responsibility—more than he or she should, in some cases. This child may begin acting like a parent to the other kids and provide help and support in other ways. He or she will have trouble relinquishing this powerful role. Dealing with this situation requires a great deal of sensitivity, negotiation, cooperation, and talking. For example:

> "I know you enjoyed all the responsibility you had, and now that Joe is here, you feel dethroned or kicked out—like an old shoe almost. I don't want you to feel that way, but it will be difficult for all of us to adjust to a new family structure. Please bear with us and keep talking to us about how you feel. We will need your help. We don't want to make this difficult for you."

Another problem in households in which there is a stepparent is *what to call the new stepparent*. Many teenagers do not want to call the stepparent "Mom" or "Dad." It is important to make it clear that they can choose their own way of addressing the stepparent.

Some may prefer to call the stepparent "Mom" or "Dad," but feel that this would be disloyal to the natural mother or father. If talking to everyone concerned helps—fine. But the final decision should be the child's.

The most common solution is to call the stepparent by his or her first name. Very angry teenagers may use "Mr. X" or "Mrs. X." Don't fight this; just work hard at alleviating fears and building communication.

Playing one parent against the other is another common problem in all families, but it is particularly difficult in families in which there is a stepparent. The only solution is not to allow it to happen.

The most interesting example of this behavior occurs when children run to the stepparent complaining about their natural parent. The stepparent usually feels pleased about being seen as an ally, so it is difficult not to play the "good-guy" (stepparent) versus the "bad-guy" (natural parent) role. If the stepparent has assumed a favorite aunt or uncle role, mentioned earlier, this behavior is much more likely to occur. It is not necessarily bad. In fact, it can enhance the relationships with the stepchildren, and it can provide a real opportunity to defuse potentially explosive battles between the children and the natural parent. However, it takes a skilled, sensitive stepparent to recognize when a good thing is becoming an uneven battle. As a stepparent, how can you tell whether this approach is turning sour?

1. Do you find yourself criticizing your husband or wife (the natural parent) while talking with the children? In other words, instead of listening to the children and letting them talk, are you agreeing with their complaints and adding a few criticisms of your own?

2. Do you find yourself sticking up for a child who is being disciplined by the natural parent? "Mary, don't be so hard on Jeff" (while Jeff is listening). "Tom, I think Joe can come in at 2 A.M. Don't be such a stick-in-the mud." "Why does Ellen have to clean her room every week?" (again while Ellen can hear the "support"). These are statements that *might* be made privately, but should never be made in front of the child.

3. Do you find yourself becoming angry with your husband or wife after listening to the kids' complaints? Do you find yourself losing respect for your spouse or becoming self-righteously critical?

4. Are you beginning to feel like a go-between? Do you promise the kids to talk to the natural parent, to relay their messages, or to try to change the natural parent? Do you carry messages back from the natural parent— messages that should be communicated directly? "Your dad says that if you cut the grass without being asked every week, you can stay out until 1 A.M. on Saturday night."

If things like this are happening in your family, it is best to reevaluate your listening role before real trouble ensues. Abrupt changes can confuse your stepchildren unnecessarily, however. Ease into your new approach gently and with an explanation:

> "I'm pleased that you trust me enough to come and talk. I like talking with you a lot. But when you have a problem with your mother, I feel it is important that she be a part of the discussion. I'm sure you wouldn't want to place me in a go-between role. Why don't we take a look at what you might want to tell her, and how?"

Stepchildren Relationships

There are a number of possibilities here:

1. The children of both remarried parents live in the same house. This is called a *blended family*.
2. The stepchildren come to visit for a day, for a week, or for the summer.
3. Both remarried parents have children from a former marriage, as well as a new baby of their own: "yours, mine, and ours."

The blended family probably calls for the greatest amount of ingenuity, patience, and creativity. If you like your spouse's children and your own and if all these children are fairly free of problems, are cooperative, and like one another, you should expect only a moderately difficult time. If any of these factors are lacking, the difficulty increases.

If the kids can't stand each other, the situation is only slightly different from that in other families. *Keep out of their fights*. Nothing can destroy a marriage faster than "me and my kids" against "you and your kids." It is not a great deal better when you punish your own kids for starting a fight with the stepchildren. Just stay out of the fight. Having separate bedrooms for the children might help, as can family meetings where gripes are aired without anger and accusations; try anything you can think of to reduce the friction, short of trying to referee.

Visiting stepchildren pose similar problems. In this situation, however, the stepparent can have an even harder time than in the blended-family situation, perhaps because the children are visiting and this "unnatural" atmosphere creates additional stresses.

It is more likely that the natural parent will engage in winning-over behavior during a visit. There may be little or no disciplining, which creates havoc, especially if there are other children in the home who live there year round. The stepparent and his or her children may feel abandoned, treated unfairly, and really put upon.

It is also common for a stepparent to just plain dislike the visiting children. They can have any number of faults that all normal kids have, but somehow these less-than-perfect stepchildren who come to visit always look worse than any other kids in the world.

The reasons for this reaction differ from person to person, but there are some common ones. They are difficult reasons to accept, though, because to some they appear petty. Nothing that is real and hurtful is petty, however. These reasons include:

1. The stepchildren are living, walking proof of the love your husband or wife had for another person.
2. If you are normal, you are not overly crazy about your husband's or wife's former spouse. He or she is currently raising these stepchildren. No wonder they're such brats!
3. Your spouse seems to love these kids so much and also appears to resent or dislike yours at times. So you think: "Maybe he still loves his ex-wife. Maybe his love for the kids will draw him back to her." That kind of thinking, if allowed to continue, will definitely make the stepchildren seem less than desirable.

"Yours, mine, and ours" is also a difficult situation, especially if they all live under the same roof. The new baby (ours) can be *very* hard for the other kids to take.

A new baby can cause problems in any family. In a family with a stepparent or in a blended family, the problems can be compounded by a very common feeling: "This new baby will be more important than I am because this baby is *theirs*. I'm only half theirs." A lot of tender loving care and deep sensitivity to your children (and also your stepchildren) are necessary to reassure them of your love and of their importance to you. This is necessary whether your children are living with you or with your former spouse. It is a difficult time for children and adolescents, and the older they are, the more embarrassing it is for them to talk about it. So, as the parent, you need to take the lead in discussions and reassurances. Your efforts can make the arrival of the new baby a positive experience rather than a traumatic one.

SECTION II

Building Communication

Chapter 8

Communication Skills

There are good ways to say things, and there are bad ways to say them. There are ways that will elicit cooperation, and there are ways that will create another war. Books on communication skills abound. Classes, seminars, and weekend workshops teach communication skills. All these are good sources for learning. Most of us are not born with these skills; we must learn them. And when we learn them well, living with adolescents—or anyone else, for that matter—is much easier.

However, frequently the biggest problem is not that you lack knowledge of communication skills but rather that you *do not want* to communicate better with your kids. Yelling, screaming, putting the other person down, and being cold and unreasonable are choices that parents and teenagers make. These choices are made for specific reasons which are not always apparent. Let's talk about some of those reasons.

When teenagers are experiencing severe communication problems, I listen carefully and empathize with their plight. Then I might ask them whether they want the fighting, or whatever the problem is, to stop. "Yes," they say. I then explain two or three simple things they can do which will almost guarantee improvement within a week at most. They are nothing spectacular, and probably these teenagers have thought of them many times before. In about eight cases out of ten, their response is "Yes, but. . . ."

"Yes, but you don't know how bad my parents are."

"Yes, but I don't think that will help."

"Yes, but I don't know if I can do that."

"Yes, but that would be hard."

The "Yes, buts. . . . " go on forever; the rest of the sentence is not important. "Yes, but. . . . " is a polite way of saying:

> "I do not want to do it. *I will not do it.* I want someone to understand me and take my side and realize how tough life is for me. But don't tell me I can change the situation. I don't really want to change it, and if you had any sensitivity, you would understand that and feel sorry for me instead of offering solutions that I know about already."

Maintaining the fight with parents usually has one of several purposes:

- To separate from the parents
- To get back at the parents for actual or supposed wrong-doing
- To get attention that is hard to get in more productive ways

But this book is for parents, not teenagers. It has been my experience that parents use "Yes, but. . . . " even more than their children. However, it is much more difficult for parents to admit the purpose of the fighting. Fighting is *never* a one-sided affair. It takes the cooperation of at least two people. Teenagers frequently admit that they fight to get revenge or for other reasons. Parents, however, do an amazing job of hiding the purpose of their fighting, sometimes even from themselves. Parents who are really interested in improving communication with their teenagers should pay close attention to the reasons for fighting discussed in this chapter. It is possible that some parents will see themselves in one of the examples. Others will need therapeutic intervention to come to a viable self-understanding.

WHY PARENTS FIGHT
WITH THEIR TEENAGERS

Reason 1: "I want to hurt and punish my teenager."

When children are little, you can send them to their rooms, keep them in the yard, or even hit them hard on the seat of the pants until they cry. You may not help the child a great deal with these actions, but at least you can act out your anger. We feel relief and satisfaction when we hurt someone who has hurt or angered us. This is called *revenge*, and most parents are embarrassed to admit that they want revenge. It is hardly the loftiest of human emotions, but it is real, and the desire for revenge is fairly common.

Once children are too old, too big, or too insolent to hit physically, parents occasionally resort to psychological hitting—putting them down, creating an atmosphere of constant tension, and even using hateful epithets. It's a way of hurting someone who is now bigger than you are.

What makes the situation worse, however, is the fact that teenagers who are subjected to such psychological beatings usually do not run off into a corner and cry. No matter how hurt they may be, either they will act tough and indifferent, or they will retaliate with similar put-downs. Acting tough makes the parents madder, and the craziness is intensified. Retaliation results in a renewed onslaught by the parents because they now have to "get back" for additional wrongs. It's a vicious, cruel cycle that either party can stop by choosing to practice new behaviors. Even if it takes six months, isn't it worth it?

Reason 2: "I don't like my teenager."

Even wanting revenge is easier to admit than this. How can you not like your child? Easy! Basically, it comes from developing an adversary position and focusing on all his or her negative attributes rather than the positive ones. In any case, it's really hard to like someone you are fighting with constantly.

Reason 3: "If I talk and act nice, my teenager wins."

Living with your adolescent has become a high-stakes poker game. Who can outsmart the other? Who can win? Having fun together and talking normally become almost impossible. Every word is analyzed for possible intent to hurt or for signs of weakness. It is impossible to relax. The purpose is to win, to defeat, to come out with all the chips so that your teenager is sure to realize who is better, superior, and smarter.

Your best friend tells you what a great listener you are. Your neighbor can't believe how helpful and understanding you are. Even your spouse, who rarely marvels at anything, thinks you are the most empathetic person around.

Then you talk to your teenager, and something strange happens. You have to be on guard, watch every step, and prepare a defense even while your son or daughter is speaking. You don't listen at all. You just try to keep thinking faster than your teenager so that he or she won't put anything over on you. It goes something like this:

> *Roger:* Mom, I just don't know what to do about that class. It seems the harder I work, the less I understand.
>
> *Mother:* Well, that doesn't make much sense. How could you possibly get behind if you're studying as hard as you can. Maybe you should quit your job.

Good old Mom, whose shoulder everyone cries on, becomes a veritable block of steel: "He's not doing well? Then the answer must be to study more. Mothers are supposed to see to it that their kids study. Anyhow, he's probably just preparing me for a bad grade, and I'm not going to be hoodwinked like that."

Roger will go away more frustrated than ever and will make a mental note not to talk to his mother again. At first he just had the class to worry about; now his mother wants him to quit his job! The situation has gone from bad to worse.

Reason 4: "If the fighting stops, how will I keep my spouse involved with me?"

Some couples say they stay together for the sake of the kids. More commonly it is a child—frequently a teenager—who keeps the parents together by acting out, fighting with them, or doing anything else that keeps them involved with each other. The "bad" kid provides a topic of conversation, does things that make it necessary for the parents to rally their resources, and is a common enemy or thorn in the side. If they can't share anything else, at least these parents can share pain. This isn't very strong glue, however, so the campaign to spur the teenager into fights or other wrongdoing continues unrelentingly.

When the "bad" kid finally moves out, this creates a crisis, so usually another child will assume the role. And the cycle goes on until there are no more children left.

This particular purpose for fighting is very common, but it is very difficult for parents to recognize it in their own situations. Therapeutic intervention is frequently necessary to help parents become aware of the pattern and then do something about it.

Reason 5: "Woe is me; look at the way I suffer."

Some people feel unimportant if no one feels sorry for them. Mouthy, insolent teenagers are always good for a lot of sympathy, so some parents cooperate in the fighting with their kids in order to have a list of injustices for public display.

Once you realize the reason for your fighting or your poor communication patterns, either through self-reflection or through therapy, you can decide whether you want the situation to continue. Is changing worth it? Will you be worse off if you stop fighting? What decision should you make?

If you decide to continue the fighting, at least you are being a bit more honest about the problem. If you decide to stop, you are choosing to break a habit—never an easy undertaking, but definitely possible. Any pattern of behavior that was learned can be unlearned. No one is too old to change or too anything to change. It's a matter of choice, decision, and lots of practice. It will take time, but most parents feel it's worth the effort.

Communication will improve when you want it to, as long as your teenager is not strung out on drugs or seriously disturbed. A normal teenager does not need to decide to stop fighting at the same time you do. If you stop, he or she has no choice.

> ***Your adolescent cannot force you to do what you don't want to do.***

So let us assume that you really want to communicate better. Not only do you want to know what to say and how to say it, but you are also willing to spend a lot of time and effort practicing this behavior.

COMMUNICATION SKILLS THAT CAN HELP YOU STOP FIGHTING

Really listening is the most important communication skill there is. *Listening* in this context means really understanding what the other person is saying and having the ability to communicate that understanding to the other person. It does not mean merely keeping quiet or hearing the words. The following are good, workable ways of communicating understanding.

Skill 1: Encouraging more talk

Sometimes the nicest, most helpful thing you can do is to encourage your adolescent to tell you more—in a sympathetic or interested tone of voice. Another way to encourage someone to talk more is to lean forward slightly and keep silent in anticipation of hearing more. Saying "mm-hum" is closest to remaining silent and also encourages more talking.

Skill 2: Making self-disclosures

"Yes, I know; sometimes I feel very lonely too." Teenagers are astounded by such honesty. They frequently don't believe their parents have experienced anything close to what they are going through: "I was 18 when I first fell in love. When she broke up with me, I felt so bad I thought I was going to die. I didn't eat or sleep much for a week."

Make your self-disclosures *brief* and discreet, and don't include a lesson or a sermon, but don't avoid revealing your humanness.

Skill 3: Restating what was said

Encouraging someone to keep talking helps that person feel you are interested. Restating what he or she said helps the individual feel that you understand.

Restating is merely repeating or summarizing the most significant part of what was said in slightly different words. Someone who is really upset, for instance, may talk all over the place for a few minutes. Summarizing what that person said communicates understanding, but it also helps the individual focus on the real issues and get a better perspective. For example:

Sally: Jane came up to me in the hall and said she wouldn't be my friend anymore because she thinks I talked about her to Kenneth. I never did that, and if I lose Jane, I won't have any friends.

Father: Someone lied about you, and now you may lose your best friend.

Jerry: Every morning I go to that class, and two or three guys tease me about one thing or another. Most of the time, I just say nothing and eat it—you know. But today I yelled back at them and Kevin, the jerk, grabbed my shirt, so I pushed him. Then the teacher came in, and I got into trouble because he didn't see Kevin grab me.

Father: You tried to defend yourself and got in trouble in the process.

Obviously, it is important to avoid mouthing the very same words back. Parroting is aggravating. Restating, reflecting feelings, and other important communication skills are for *occasional* use when listening and understanding are important. Constant use in ordinary conversations could become repugnant.

Skill 4: Reflecting feelings

Reflecting feelings is without a doubt the best way to communicate understanding. It is also difficult for most people to learn. But with continued effort, anyone can become good at it. At first, it will feel clumsy, even manipulative, as you fumble for the right words. But one day, you will suddenly realize that you have just reflected feelings without even thinking about it. It is no longer a technique; it has become a part of you.

Following are examples of statements that teenagers make about common situations or problems; typical responses, as well as a reflection of feeling, are given after each one. Try hard to place yourself in the shoes of the teenager in each example. Which response would you prefer?

Example 1: School

    George: Dad, math is so hard, I can hardly believe it. But the worst of it is that everyone else seems to understand it. And Miss Bara, my English teacher, piled on so much homework; she should be teaching college or something. And I have to keep my grade point average up.

TYPICAL RESPONSE A

    Father: Well, George, you will just have to stay in on weekends and get that work done.

    George: Yeah, but that won't help.

TYPICAL RESPONSE B

Father: Maybe you should drop one of your classes.

George: Oh, I can't do that!

TYPICAL RESPONSE C

Father: It should get better next week. Nothing can be that bad for long.

George: I'm not so sure.

BETTER RESPONSE: REFLECTION OF FEELING

Father: Sometimes you just feel overwhelmed, and the pressure really builds up.

George: Yeah, it sure does! Sometimes I just think I can't handle it, but then if I talk about it, it helps a lot. Like just now I'm thinking about asking Larry to explain one part to me. If I could get that one section, I'd be home free with a couple of weeks' work.

Example 2: Friends

Tom: Joe and Charlie went to the movies last night and didn't even ask me. I mean, we've been friends for years, and all of a sudden I get something like this.

TYPICAL RESPONSE A

Mother: Maybe you should just find new friends.

Tom: No, Ma, that's not the point.

TYPICAL RESPONSE B

Mother: You'll get a lot more studying done if you don't hang around them so much.

Tom: (silence)

TYPICAL RESPONSE C

Mother: Oh, you poor dear. How can anyone be so mean?

Tom: Oh, they're not mean. Oh—never mind.

BETTER RESPONSE: REFLECTION OF FEELING

> *Mother:* You really feel rejected—kind of kicked in the stomach.
>
> *Tom:* I sure do. I'm not really sure what to say to them either. I don't think they realize how they can hurt me sometimes.

Example 3: Home

The hair dryer has just breathed its last, it's 7 A.M., the bus arrives in half an hour, and Sue has just washed her hair:

> *Sue: Ma!* The hair dryer isn't working!

TYPICAL RESPONSE A

> *Mother:* Well, I didn't break it. Don't yell at me.

TYPICAL RESPONSE B

> *Mother:* No wonder. You've got it on half the day.

TYPICAL RESPONSE C

> *Mother:* I'll heat the oven. You can get it dry in there.
>
> *Sue:* I don't have to get it *dry*; I have to *style* it!

BETTER RESPONSE: REFLECTION OF FEELING

> *Mother:* It is *very* frustrating to have something break down when you need it the most.
>
> *Sue:* You can say that again! Wow, what should I do? How about Jennie's next door? She's up, and I'm sure she wouldn't mind. I'll be right back.

When you reflect feelings, you look *beyond the words to the feelings expressed*. Ask yourself: "If I had said that, how would I probably *feel*?" You are not dealing with thoughts, reason, or anything else in that category. You are concerned with how the person *feels*. Reflecting this feeling conveys a real empathy and understanding and helps the individual deal with small or big things in much more productive, constructive ways. It also helps defuse negative feelings and enhance positive ones.

"Friends halve our sorrow and double our joy." That's what reflecting feelings does too.

Use the technique judiciously, but do use it. It can produce remarkable results. If you are reflecting feelings correctly and at appropriate times, the other person will never realize what you are doing. He or she will simply feel understood and very good about talking to you. Overuse will create irritation, so you will quickly learn how much is too much.

As parents, we have a tendency to try to solve all problems, provide answers, and give advice. This near compulsion for instant solutions gets in the way of our really listening. We *can't* solve all our children's problems, and neither can they, but we can listen so that they feel understood. Once they feel understood, they are in a much better frame of mind to solve their own problems.

Now read the following examples, decide what the dominant feelings are, and think up a response. Possible answers are given at the end of this chapter. The responses are merely suggestions. There are many, many others that would also reflect feelings quite well. So if your responses do not match these, it does not necessarily mean they are wrong. If your responses show that you have guessed how the other person feels, you are off to a great start. Remember, though, that this is difficult, so don't get discouraged. It takes time and practice.

Practice 1

I was fired today. The new store took all the business away, so now I have to start looking for a job all over again. I'll never find one this good again.

Feelings: _____

Response: _____

Practice 2

Mom, all I've done for this new girl is show her around school and stuff like that, but today she brought me a rose and said I was one of the nicest people she has ever met!

Feelings: _____

Response: _____

Practice 3

So I went to the hospital, but she was in such pain that I just didn't know what to do. When I asked her what I could do, she just said, "Nothing, really."

Feelings: _____

Response: _____

Practice 4

I don't know whether I should go to college. I wouldn't know what to major in.

Feelings: _____

Response: _____

Practice 5

If I do my homework, it's usually wrong, so the teacher tells me to do it over. If I don't do it, she yells at me and takes off points.

Feelings: _____

Response: _____

Practice 6

He walked up to me and said he was going to beat me up. I don't know why or anything. He just wants to beat me up. I can't ever go back to school.

Feelings: _____

Response: _____

Suggested Answers

Practice 1

Feelings: Dejected, discouraged, and somewhat apprehensive

POSSIBLE RESPONSES
1. It's really a letdown when you lose a job you like so much.
2. It's a real pain to have to start looking for a job all over again.
3. It's a little scary wondering if you'll find another job, let alone one that's as good as that one.

Practice 2

Feelings: Very good, warm, useful, and appreciated

POSSIBLE RESPONSES
1. You just feel warm and good all over, don't you?
2. It's such a great feeling when others appreciate us.
3. How great! This girl has really made you feel good about yourself.

Practice 3

Feelings: Helpless, sad, and perhaps frustrated

POSSIBLE RESPONSES
1. You must feel helpless.
2. It's really sad not to be able to help someone you love.

Practice 4

Feelings: Confused, undecided, and anxious

POSSIBLE RESPONSES
1. It's really scary and confusing not knowing what you want to do.
2. You're feeling a lot of pressure to decide, aren't you?

Practice 5

Feelings: Frustrated and discouraged

POSSIBLE RESPONSES
1. You just can't win.
2. It must be terribly frustrating going to that class each day just to be put down.

Practice 6

Feelings: Fearful and confused

POSSIBLE RESPONSES
1. It must be frightening having this gorilla in the same school.
2. Sometimes it's really hard to know how to deal with bullies.

More opportunities to practice this skill are provided in the next two chapters.

Chapter 9

Other Responses to Develop or Avoid

DEVELOP RESPONSES THAT HELP

Good communication consists first and foremost of listening well enough so that you can feed back the content and feeling of what you have heard and, as a consequence, make the other person feel understood. However, there are also other ways of responding that can go a long way toward enhancing your communication with your adolescent and helping your son or daughter feel that he or she is a worthwhile, loved individual.

Helpful Response 1: Accept the person, if not the behavior

There are two primary reasons why this is difficult. First, a child finds it hard to feel loved and accepted if 95 percent of what he or she does is criticized and if the parents never say anything positive. Second, if you see only negative things in someone, it is difficult to continue liking that person. And if you really don't like your son or daughter, it is almost impossible to hide that feeling. The only recourse is to concentrate on the positive. This will help you like your son or daughter again, and it will probably help change his or her behavior for the better.

The next chapter, which deals with encouragement, may be of some assistance. In addition, it is important to choose angry words carefully. Following are some typical responses and suggested alternatives:

> *Typical Response:* You're a rotten kid. How could you lie to us like that?
>
> *Alternative:* It makes *me* very angry when you lie to us. *I feel* betrayed and distant from you.

> *Typical Response:* How do you possibly expect to get into college with grades like this? You're just a failure.
>
> *Alternative:* When you continue to bring home poor grades, it frightens *me*. *I'm afraid* you eventually won't be able to get a job you *like*. *I care* what happens to you, so that possibility is scary.

Helpful Response 2: Use "I" statements

Realize that you control your feelings, your thoughts, and your perceptions. Have you ever found yourself saying, "You make me so angry"? No one can make you angry. You choose to become angry under certain conditions with certain people. Little is gained by accusing another person of creating a feeling that is within your control.

For instance, let us assume that you are angry because your son is ten minutes late. You had agreed on a time to meet, and now you have to sit and wait. When he shows up, you lash out in anger: "You stupid, inconsiderate brat! I said five o'clock, and it's already ten minutes after."

Would your response be the same if your husband was ten minutes late? If you already fight about everything, perhaps it would. But it is more likely that you would say, "What kept you?" What if a friend is ten minutes late? The chances are you don't think a thing about it. The point is that waiting ten minutes is something you can choose to get angry about if you wish to. Therefore, a more appropriate response might be: *"I get angry* when I have to wait for you." Here's another example:

> *Typical Response:* You're impossible. I asked you to clean the front room, and look at that mess.
>
> *Alternative:* When I ask you to clean and you don't do it, *I become* very *frustrated* and *disgusted.*

The typical response will just alienate your teenager further and will almost guarantee a repeat performance of the undesirable behavior. The alternative response is honest and doesn't judge the other person. Your son or daughter can even identify with it. Other examples are as follows:

> *Typical Response:* You make me look like a jerk.
>
> *Alternative:* When you don't even introduce me to the friends you bring into the house, *I feel* as if you're ashamed of me.

> *Typical Response:* You seem to enjoy hurting me.
>
> *Alternative:* *I feel* very sad when you say hurtful things. *I feel* as if I've failed miserably.

Helpful Response 3: *Invite independence*

Although adolescents crave independence, they are also frightened by it. Parents are frequently willing to alleviate the fear by making decisions for their kids. But dependence creates hostility, so a parent who is interested in helping an adolescent grow and feel better about himself or herself is advised to practice a repertoire of "independence" statements. Some examples follow; you can probably think of many more:

"I'm confident you can make a good decision."

"It is difficult to decide which way to go, but whichever way you choose is fine with me."

"It's up to you."

"The choice is yours."

"Do it if you want to."

Helpful Response 4: Respect privacy

Parents should never search through rooms, pockets, or anything else that belongs to their adolescents. Some parents maintain that this is the only way they can feel they are on top of the
situation. Looking for drugs, cigarettes, and birth control devices and reading notes or letters are their way of keeping one
step ahead.

Such snooping is a very dangerous practice. The only time
it is justified is when the adolescent has been warned that the
parent will make a search after a series of very *serious* problems,
such as repeated shoplifting or burglary or heavy drug use.

But parents are advised to respect privacy in other ways as
well. If an adolescent is reluctant to talk about school, friends,
or anything else, little is gained by pumping for information.

Helpful Response 5: Be consistent

Consistency has to do with the pattern of your responses. Responding consistently is important, but it is difficult to describe.
It means that you follow through on what you promise—good
or bad. It means that the same actions, words, or attitudes will
normally elicit the same responses. It means that you rule your
moods, rather than vice versa. It means that rules don't change
rapidly or for no stated reason. It means that favoritism is kept
to a minimum.

*Be consistent by following through on what you promise and by not
promising what you can't deliver.*

Ted (age 16):	My dad grounded me for a week and took the car away for a month.
Counselor:	Then how do you expect to go to the dance this weekend?
Ted (laughing):	My parents are paper tigers. All I have to do is wait a day or two. Then I'll look real sad and mope around a lot. By Friday I won't be grounded, and they'll let me use the car.
Counselor:	You're pretty sure about that, aren't you?

Ted: Yeah, they never follow through on any-
       thing. If they try to, I just give them a
       harder time. It's a piece of cake.

Ted's parents might be described as predictable, but hardly as consistent.

There are times when parents mete out ridiculous punishment in the heat of anger and later regret their decision. If it becomes necessary to change your mind, admit your mistake: "Joe, I was very angry when I grounded you for six months. I now realize that was more a reaction to my anger than common sense. You will be grounded for two weeks."

The only way to avoid the excesses of anger is never to mete out punishment or consequences when you are angry. Even if this is difficult, force yourself to do it. Delay making a decision until you calm down so that you won't have to change horses in midstream.

Let's look at another common example: "If you ever do that again, I'm kicking you out of the house." Will you really kick him out, or is this a way to express how very angry you are? It is not true that "the kid knows I won't kick him out." He doesn't know for sure. In fact, children who are frequently threatened in this way have varied reactions that range anywhere from a feeling of rejection to panic to disgust. The parent doesn't see these reactions, however. They are well hidden because the parent and the adolescent are in a real battle, and the teenager doesn't want the parent to know how deeply he or she has been hurt. The adolescent will probably play it very cool, but may get into more trouble at home or at school and otherwise try to fight back or retain some sense of equilibrium.

Never promise what you won't or can't do. Once you promise something, follow through.

Be consistent by responding to the same behavior in the same way.

Claudia: I never know what to expect. On some days, I can
     bring friends over and my mother is kind and

friendly. Other days, she will be rude and even kick them out. I would rather have her say I can never bring them over than not know what will happen when I do.

Clifford: When I work hard, I can get C's and a few B's. I've been getting these grades for years. But when the report cards come home, there is no way of knowing how my father will react. Sometimes he ignores them totally, other times he tells me how well I'm doing, and other times he gets himself into a real fit about how dumb I am. In fact, he got the maddest with one of my better report cards.

It would be better for Clifford if his father yelled every time than if he continues reacting so inconsistently. Even though yelling about an adequate report card is not good, inconsistency is worse. Clifford has no idea where he stands with his father.

Be consistent by ruling your moods.

Eugenia: I hate going home after school. I never know what mood my mother will be in. One day she is bubbly and friendly, and the next day she is ready to kill me for heaven knows what. I would almost rather she were rotten every day. At least I would know what to expect and could deal with it better.

Obviously, all of us have bad days. It is impossible to be a perfectly even-tempered person. Adolescents don't expect that any more than anyone else does. But radical mood swings that dramatically affect a parent's responses are detrimental to a teenager.

Be consistent by not changing rules arbitrarily. After reading this book, it is possible that you will want to make some changes in the way you deal with your teenager. But these changes should be thought out, deliberate, and explained. Being consistent does not mean never changing; it means avoiding a flip-flop situation in which you keep changing back and forth with such rapidity that other family members cannot maintain their equilibrium.

Keith: My parents and I have agreed on a time for me to be in on weekends, and I never try to take advantage. I'm always in by midnight. Sometimes it's fine, but half the time my father gets all bent out of shape when I come in *on time*. I have asked him what the problem is, but he won't tell me. He doesn't change his mind about when I have to be home, but he gets mad when I come in then. I can't win.

Tim: My Dad has been complaining for months about how I dress. My clothes were too old, too dirty, too tight, or too messy. I never looked right. So I finally got a part-time job and went out and bought a few nice shirts and cords. Yesterday I got all dressed up and came downstairs to show off. Do you want to know what he said? "How much money did you waste on those clothes?" I was really hurt, but I told him I used my own money. Then he got even madder. I'm going nuts living in that house. It's like going through a haunted house and expecting someone to jump out or hurt you any minute.

Gerry: My mother is driving me crazy. She said I had to be home for supper at 5:30. I was there four days in a row, and we didn't eat until 6. But I still came home at 5:30. So yesterday they started eating at 5:15, and she was mad because I wasn't there. She didn't tell me to be home at 5:15.

This kind of thing goes on all the time. Parents who are inconsistent with even the simplest rules are inviting rebellion. No one can live and grow in an atmosphere of chaos. The only protection the young person has is total separation. This is most often accomplished by becoming rebellious, running away, or both.

Be consistent by keeping favoritism to a minimum. It is impossible for parents to treat all their children alike. Each one is an individual with individual needs and an individual personality. Parents have favorites, and children can immediately identify which is the mother's favorite, which is the father's favorite, and even which is the grandmother's favorite. There isn't much that can be done about that. But blatant, obvious, unfair favoritism is harmful to everyone concerned.

Inconsistency in any form is harmful to all family members. A more than normal amount causes confusion, frustration, and anger. It also makes parents look ridiculous in their own children's eyes. A lot of inconsistency over a long period can cause serious psychological harm, ranging from alienation from parents to severe insecurity or worse.

What else can you do if inconsistency is still a problem?

Helpful Hint 1: Never promise good things that probably won't happen

In an effort to make children feel better or to make up to them for actual or supposed injustices, or just because it's easier for the moment, some parents promise the moon. It's better to surprise adolescents with something good than to promise what you can't be sure of delivering.

Helpful Hint 2: Examine your behavior to see in what area you are most inconsistent

Then take a month or longer and work on just that area. Don't try to change everything overnight. If you can change one response that you don't like, that is wonderful.

Helpful Hint 3: Don't be so hard on yourself

It has been my experience that parents who admit they are inconsistent frequently act out of guilt rather than reason. The flip-flop behavior comes from alternating between cracking down and trying to make up for cracking down.

If it is necessary for you to crack down, then do it for the good of you and your child, and don't feel guilty about it. Your adolescent is probably good at making you feel guilty. Just refuse to feel the pressure. Expect that it will come, but decide ahead of time how you will resist it.

AVOID RESPONSES THAT DON'T HELP

Haim Ginot, in *Between Parent and Teenager*, gives a wonderful list of responses to avoid. The following examples also provide good practice for making more appropriate responses. Write down how you would restate each response and reflect the feeling. Sample responses appear at the end of this section.

Unhelpful Response 1: Reasoning

Example A

> *Teenager:* Well, I want to work, but I also want to do well in school and be on the football team.
>
> *Parent:* You can't do two things at the same time, and there are only twenty-four hours in a day.

> *Restatement:* _____
> *Reflection of Feeling:* _____

Unhelpful Response 2: Using Clichés

Example B

> *Teenager:* I was sure I was going to get an A. I just can't believe I didn't.
>
> *Parent:* I hope that will teach you not to count your chickens before they're hatched.

Restatement: _____

Reflection of Feeling: _____

Unhelpful Response 3: Preaching

Preaching is not always effective even from the pulpit. It is even less effective in interpersonal relationships. An especially boring form of preaching begins with, "When I was your age. . . ." And preaching spiked with chichés is guaranteed to prompt rolling eyes in the listener.

Example C

Teenager: All the other kids have What's In jeans. I wish I could get just one pair when you can afford it.

Parent: Young lady, it's about time you learned the value of a dollar. I just bought you jeans last month; I'm sure not going to buy What's In jeans just because other people are crazy enough to waste their money on them. Money doesn't grow on trees, you know.

Restatement: _____

Reflection of Feeling: _____

Example D

Teenager: The coldest day of the year, and that bus was half an hour late.

Parent: When I was your age, I walked 3 miles to school. Rain, cold, snow. . . .

Restatement: _____

Reflection of Feeling: _____

Unhelpful Response 4: Minimizing the situation

Minimizing a situation can create a great deal of anger. It means that the other person's perceptions are being questioned. Parents believe it will help by placing the situation in perspective or reducing its impact. That is almost always not true.

Example E

> *Teenager:* I *have* to make the football team. I can't even study worrying about it.
>
> *Parent:* Why should playing a game in which people get their kicks by hurting each other be so important? Big deal. It wouldn't be any great loss.

Restatement: _____

Reflection of Feeling: _____

Unhelpful Response 5: Criticizing personal characteristics

Statements in this category almost always begin, "The trouble with you is. . . ."

Example F

> *Teenager:* I hate doing homework.
>
> *Parent:* The trouble with you is that you have never learned how to discipline yourself. You think you can do anything you want. You're in for a rude awakening, because the real world isn't like that.

Restatement: _____

Reflection of Feeling: _____

Unhelpful Response 6: Pitying or being too understanding

At first glance, such a response appears to be better than the preceding examples of unhelpful responses. Actually, in most cases, it is worse. Overprotection is almost always worse than just plain meanness. A pampered child never grows up, and that is more disabling than going through adolescence with more than an average share of anger and trouble. Furthermore, no one can know exactly how anyone else feels. Parents who say that they do are implying that their teenagers are transparent and naive and are experiencing something that is very ordinary. Even if this is true, saying it is a put-down. Reflecting feelings can communicate some understanding, but saying "I know exactly how you feel" is deprecating and a turn-off.

Example G

> *Teenager:* I applied for that job before Jenny, and she got it instead of me.
>
> *Parent:* Oh, you must feel terrible. How unfair! Some people have connections I guess, and we have none at all. How sad that life has to be this way.

Restatement: _____

Reflection of Feeling: _____

Example H

> *Teenager:* We've been going out for five months, and now she just walks off. I feel so bad, I could die.
>
> *Parent:* You poor thing. I know exactly how you feel.

Restatement: _____

Reflection of Feeling: _____

Unhelpful Response 7: Futurizing

Futurizing is a valiant attempt to save your child from some possible future woe. Typical futurizing statements are:

> "You're too close to Fred. When you go off to college, you won't know what to do with yourself."
>
> "If you don't get better grades, you'll be a failure."
>
> "I don't want you to have a dog because if it gets killed, you'll be all upset."

Example I

> *Teenager:* I really want to go away to college, and I've saved enough money to pay for it.
>
> *Parent:* It isn't really a good idea. You'll be homesick and have to drop out before the end of the first semester.

Restatement: _____

Reflection of Feeling: _____

Sample Responses

See how many of your restatements and reflections of feelings are similar to those given below or better. Then try practicing your new or improved skills in actual situations.

Example A

> *Restatement:* It's difficult to decide how to use your time.
>
> *Reflection of Feeling:* It's frustrating sometimes when you are afraid you can't do everything you want to do.

Example B

> *Restatement:* Everything pointed to an A.
>
> *Reflection of Feeling:* What a letdown!

Example C

> *Restatement:* You're the only one without What's In jeans.
>
> *Reflection of Feeling:* You feel a little deprived because other kids have What's In jeans and you don't.

Example D

Restatement: A freezing day, and no bus!

Reflection of Feeling: You must have been ready to give up and come home. But you didn't. That must make you feel kind of proud.

Example E

Restatement: Making the team is very important to you.

Reflection of Feeling: When you want something very badly, it's scary to know you may not get it.

Example F

Restatement: Homework is no fun.

Reflection of Feeling: Yeah, sometimes it's the pits having to do something you don't enjoy.

Example G

Restatement: You got an application in early and still didn't get the job.

Reflection of Feeling: Sometimes job hunting is discouraging. It almost seems unfair at times.

Example H

Restatement: You had five good months, and the relationship is ending.

Reflection of Feeling: It really hurts when someone you like so much rejects you.

Example I

Restatement:	Going away to college is something you want and have really planned for.
Reflection of Feeling:	You really need to get out on your own, and you're proud of having worked so hard for it.

AVOID FEELINGS THAT DON'T HELP

Guilt

I spoke about guilt in Chapter 7 in connection with single parents; however, guilt is such a big issue that further discussion is necessary. Somehow, parents have been led to believe that when something goes wrong with their kids, it's the parents' fault. The people at school and relatives and neighbors never really accuse you, but you have the distinct feeling that when all is said and done, they are thinking, "If you were all right, your kid would be all right."

Since you feel everyone else thinks that, you begin thinking it too:

"What could I have done differently?"

"My wife's too mean; that must be it."

"If I were home more, this wouldn't have happened."

"Maybe we should have gotten psychological help when he was 3."

Now you are reading this book, which is giving you all kinds of ideas about how to change your behavior. So you think, "If I have to change, there must be something wrong with me." Wrong!

Don't assign blame. Why does anyone have to be at fault? It is very helpful if you can feel less need to find the cause of a problem: "What made her become depressed?" "Why is he a problem child?" No one *really* knows. Plenty of people want to make guesses, and perhaps the guesses are even partially correct, but what good does this do? Trying to assign blame serves no good purpose. What can assigning blame possibly accomplish? The problem exists today. It takes far too much time and energy to wail about what should have been. The past is past. What do you do today? That's the important question.

No one is perfect, and some of us are less perfect than others. Let us assume that you have read through the sections on communication and have decided that you have done it all wrong for fourteen years. Maybe someone else has always felt that he was the perfect father—had excellent communication skills and so forth—but discovers that he has been so overprotective that his 28-year-old is still very immature and shows no sign of ever leaving the house. There is no need to blame yourself for poor communication skills or overprotectiveness or anything else. If you want to learn to communicate better, work on that at your own pace. If you want to be less protective, work on that. Today and tomorrow are all you have. Yesterday is past. Don't waste time regretting it. *None* of us are perfect parents. *None* of our children are perfect children.

The difference between conditions and fault: Imagine that you are driving your car carefully and at the speed limit. A child darts out in front of you, and the impact seriously injures the child. You are horrified: "How could this have happened? If I had left two minutes earlier or later. . . . If I had made the light at the last intersection. . . . If I had stayed in today. . . . If. . . . If. . . ." The point is that the conditions were just right, and there is nothing anyone can do to change the horrible reality. It's not your fault that you left at 5:05 instead of 5:09. It's not your fault that the child didn't check for cars. Nothing is your fault. The conditions were such that the accident occurred.

Imagine instead that you are speeding down a residential street at 60 miles an hour, just for fun, and a young boy runs in front of your car. Imagine that you are so angry at the child that you deliberately run him down. This is an entirely different situation.

To be human is to make mistakes. Some can't be avoided no matter how hard we try, and some could have been avoided. In some cases we actually set out to do harm. But no matter what applies to you in which circumstances, all you can do about any past mistake today is to change whatever behavior you choose to change. Yesterday is past, done, over. Start fresh today.

Being a parent is one of the most difficult jobs you will ever have, and it is the one job for which you have little or no training. Can you imagine someone putting you in front of a million-dollar computer and without one day of training saying, "OK, it's all yours. Take care of it." Essentially that's what happens when we become parents. We have no training, and we are expected to raise happy, well-adjusted children. A child is infinitely more complicated than a computer, and yet we are all expected somehow to figure out what to say and what to do on a twenty-four-hour-a-day basis. It is *impossible* to avoid making mistakes.

"I'm the only one who has these problems. Everyone else seems to have wonderful children." After reading this book, you may begin to believe that you are not the only one. Trust me—you're not. As parents, we are embarrassed when our kids aren't perfect, so we don't talk about our problems. The result is a smiling exterior and a confused and hurt inner feeling. If you feel very alone and can't shake the feeling, join a group of parents who have similar problems. Tough Love is one such group, but there may be many more in your town or city. The school and local mental health centers are the best places to begin looking for friendly, understanding faces. You need the group to confirm that you are not alone. You may also discover that your problems are quite minor compared with those of other parents you meet. You might also get wonderful ideas that apply to your situation.

Loss of hope: After many months or many years of fighting what appears to be a losing battle, parents are often tempted to give up. *Giving up* means different things to different people:

- For some it means letting adolescents do what they want. If they want to stay out all night, smoke marijuana, or steal cars, let them. The parents are through fighting.

- For others it means not talking to the adolescent as a form of punishment and self-protection.
- Other parents give up by making themselves sick, physically or mentally.

Although there are no easy answers or surefire solutions, there is too much at stake for you and your child to lose hope. Being hopeful does not mean believing in Pollyanna solutions. It means making reasonable, if difficult, efforts. Many such efforts are described in this book. It also means believing in yourself and your child. Being hopeful means doing what you can without assuming responsibility for your child's misbehavior and without feeling guilty.

Hope is generated from within and is nourished by supportive people in the neighborhood—a therapist; a priest, minister, or rabbi; a parents' group; or an individual at school who likes your child. Don't try to do it alone. Actively seek out as much support as you can.

Chapter 10

Encouragement

Restating what was said and reflecting feelings help encourage the other person. Because encouraging behaviors are so important, this chapter will develop the idea more extensively. Try to place yourself in the situations described below.

Example 1

Mary has just lost her purse, which contained $5 of her own money. She feels terrible about it.

> *Response A:* You are so careless! When will you ever be responsible enough to do anything?

(If Mary felt bad before, she now feels worse. She is really discouraged.)

> *Response B:* You poor dear. Here's another $5.

(This parent is being very overprotective. It is too bad that Mary lost the money, but it is her responsibility. There is no need for her mother or father to bail her out. Not having $5 is a natural consequence of losing it. It is too bad, but it is life. Things like that happen.)

> *Response C:* It really feels bad when you lose something you worked hard for.

(Reflecting feelings is always appropriate.)

Response D: It's really too bad that you lost the money, Mary, but it's a lot better than if you'd lost your purse yesterday, when you were carrying $20.

(Mary is not judged, and now she even sees something good about losing only $5.)

Example 2

Tim is just beginning to drive. He drives too slowly, rides the shoulder periodically, and looks as if he is glued to the steering wheel.

Response A: Step on it, Tim; you're holding up traffic.

Response B: You've got plenty of room. Don't put us in the ditch.

(These comments are guaranteed to raise Tim's anxiety level beyond the white-knuckle stage.)

Response C: Tim, you have a very good sense of distance. You seem to know exactly when to apply the brakes.

("Wow," Tim thinks, "I'm doing something right!" He relaxes a little, which improves his driving.)

Example 3

John has had a run-in with Mr. Smith, a neighbor. "Mom," he says, "I just won't apologize to Mr. Smith. I don't care if he is a neighbor; he had no right to yell at me for doing nothing. He should apologize to me."

Response A: You are so stubborn!

(This parent hasn't seen anything yet!)

Response B: It makes no difference who is at fault. You are younger and should apologize.

(This response is unfair.)

Response C: You are very strong and independent. I trust you will handle the situation well.

(Strong and independent are the flip side of stubborn. This statement helps John relax so that he can look at the situation more objectively. After making a statement like this, though, it is important for John's mother actually to trust him to handle the situation well. This means that she won't check up on him or criticize what he does.)

We will look at many more examples later in the chapter, but first it's important to know what is meant by *encouragement* and *encouraging statements*.

To encourage is literally to give courage. It enables the other person to grow, to move forward. Alfred Adler felt that this was the purpose of psychotherapy—to help an individual become courageous enough to deal effectively with the tasks of life. Rudolf Dreikurs continued the theme in his books for parents and teachers. Don Dinkmeyer and Lewis Losoncy, in *The Encouragement Book*, define it this way: "Encouragement is the process of facilitating the development of the person's inner resources and courage towards positive movement" (p. 16).

Encouragement should not be confused with praise. Although they both focus on the positive aspects of a situation, encouragement is valuable, while praise can be detrimental. Praise tends to value production rather than the person and his or her resources.

What Praise Values	**What Encouragement Values**
Production	The person
Deeds	The doer
What's on the outside	What's on the inside

Praise: That's a nice picture.

(What does that mean—"nice"?)

Encouragement: You have a fine sense of color that enhances your art.

(Gee, I guess I do. Let me try another one.)

Praise: You are such a good boy.

(What happens if I do something that isn't good? Am I then bad?)

Encouragement: It pleases me when you are so considerate to my friends.

(How many other ways can I be considerate?)

Praise also tends to set unrealistic standards. Everything must be good or great. Encouragement recognizes effort and improvement. There is much less emphasis on the finished product. There isn't the need for perfection that praise develops.

Praise: You *will* amount to something. Look at this, Alice. Our son got all A's.

(Talk about a double message! Does that mean that if I get all B's, I'll be a loser?)

Encouragement: You are very disciplined and hardworking. It must be a thrill to have that recognized with such a fine report card. It's time to celebrate—not just a great report card, but all the effort that made it possible.

(And I'm really going to keep working at it, too.)

Praise: You are so pretty.

(I'm certainly not as pretty as Jane.)

Encouragement: When you smile like that from the inside, so to speak, you're not just pretty—you make anyone who is around you feel good.

(Hey, I'm a neat person, maybe.)

Praise: You are so smart.

(I'm not as smart as Fred.)

Encouragement: I'm proud of you. You worked so hard, and you got what you wanted.

(Yeah, I did work hard, and I think I'm going to work even harder now.)

For many people, becoming an encouraging person takes a lot of practice and effort, especially when it comes to encouraging their children. There are so many factors in our society that make it easier to be discouraging.

An autocratic tradition is one of the culprits. We tend to dominate our kids by doing for them what they should be doing for themselves and by demanding obedience and performance rather than working at getting their cooperation. We immobilize and infantilize our children in these ways, but the effects are so slow and cumulative that it is difficult to realize what we are doing.

We also get caught in power struggles, especially with adolescents. Our responses are intended to allow us to get back, hurt, and stay on top. Domination is a risky way to retain power. A teenager's feeling of powerlessness breeds contempt and rebelliousness. The most damaged are those who have been stepped on so much and for so long that they never recover enough courage to lead full, productive lives.

The tendency to find faults instead of strengths is a pervasive, pessimistic habit at all levels. A pessimistic person, one who sees the negative more readily than the positive, is at a serious disadvantage in business, teaching, or parenting—in any situation in which interpersonal relationships are important.

Learning to become an encouraging person is difficult. It takes a lot of confidence, a commitment to learning, and much practice. Don't expect to do it overnight. Nothing worth striving for is ever quite that simple. There are some guidelines to help you along, but take your time—building slowly but well.

Guideline 1: Focus on resources and strengths

Would you like to know how hard this is? Take a sheet of paper and in the next two minutes list all your strengths—all the good things about you. Go ahead; try it.

How did you do? Two strengths? Five? Ten? It is very difficult to generalize about a thing like this, but I would like to make a guess. You can decide whether I am right. I would guess that if you listed two to four strengths, you have (or had) parents and probably a spouse who rarely point out what you do right and who rarely tell you that you are a worthwhile person. If you listed as many as ten strengths in a two-minute period, you are unusual. It is likely that you have a lot of self-confidence, tend to see the positive rather than the negative, and are already a very encouraging person.

Now for those of you who listed two to four strengths—how long do you think it would take you to list ten *weaknesses?* Not long, right? Someone is always pointing them out for you, so they are on the tip of your pen.

This exercise is even harder for adolescents. I have used it time and time again with all kinds of young people. Very few have been able to list ten assets or strengths in five minutes instead of the two I gave you.

Now turn the sheet of paper over and write the name of your adolescent at the top; then list all his or her strengths and assets. Take as long as you want and list as many as you can.

Need some help? A group of parents were discussing our "double-standard" vocabulary. They came up with a number of examples which demonstrate the point:

As a parent, I put off work in the house because I deserve a rest after a hard day's work.

You put off work because you're lazy.

I got poor grades in high school because I was a normal kid and the teachers were old-fashioned.

You get poor grades because you are undisciplined and immature.

I yell at you to make you behave.

You yell at me because you have not learned to behave.

I choose what to tell you because you don't have to know about my whole life.
You lie to me.

I take time to sit and evaluate my day.
You sit and daydream.

I clean carefully.
You are poky when you clean your room.

Think about how you may have applied the double standard. Now go back and see whether you can lengthen the list of your teenager's strengths.

Got the idea? Let's try some more. All those weaknesses and liabilities we see in our kids may just be diamonds in the rough.

Liability	Asset
Has angry outbursts	Is assertive; can't be pushed around
Is stubborn	Is highly principled; is strong and direct; can't be easily led astray
Acts timid and shy	Is reserved and discreet; is cautious
Can be tactless	Is honest and direct
Behaves recklessly	Is adventuresome and interesting

Now save the list. It's important; on bad days, you will have to refer to it to assure yourself that your adolescent indeed has many positive attributes.

The next step is to tell your adolescent about his or her strengths and assets. It's probably easier at first just to say something out of the blue. Then you can rehearse. Rehearsing is a good way of becoming comfortable in a new role:

"Jim, I admire your natural ability to put people at ease."

"Sally, you have a real gift for listening to people. It makes me very proud of you."

"Joe, your ability to repair almost anything is incredible. How do you do it?"

"Judy, you have such a sense for decorating. Your room looks like something in *Better Homes and Gardens*."

Making encouraging statements in actual situations comes next:

"Fred, you were so generous to that couple who stopped in today. You were under no obligation to help them out like that, but you did it willingly and cheerfully. It makes me feel good all over."

"Joan, you are always so kind and patient when Grandma comes over. I really admire that in you."

"I couldn't believe how easy the move was with you coordinating everything. What an organizer!"

Review the events of the last few days. What did your adolescent do that was evidence of a real asset? Practice finding your adolescent's strengths, and then practice telling him or her about them. Watch your adolescent smile more, walk taller, and cooperate more. It is so good to hear something encouraging that it impels any of us to do even better. It may take time, but it can make life wonderful for everyone involved.

Guideline 2: Focus on efforts and contributions

Finding strengths and assets is difficult enough sometimes, but focusing on efforts and contributions can be even harder because we feel it is our duty to demand high standards or point out deficiencies so that the other person will improve. The fact that this doesn't work rarely deters us. A few examples will illustrate the point. Put yourself in the position of the teenagers in the following examples and see which response would make you want to do even better.

Example 1

Your daughter could easily win anyone's Mess of the Year Award, but one Saturday she decides to really clean her room.

She works for a couple of hours and announces her achievement with pride. You go up there and find that she has made her bed and cleaned one corner. The rest of the room does not meet your standards.

Response A: It's still very messy.

(Now she's mad, and by noon you won't even have a made bed and a clean corner.)

Response B: The bed looks very nice, and that corner over there really looks cozy. You worked hard.

See why this is so difficult? Let's try another one.

Example 2

Your son has just cut the grass. He ran the lawn mower the wrong way and got grass clippings all over your flowers. He also left strips around the rose bed.

Response A: You forgot those strips around the roses, and the flowers are a mess now.

(This is what you see because everyone is expected to cut lawns perfectly. We are conditioned to find mistakes.)

Response B: It makes everything look better when the grass is cut well. I'm especially glad you didn't leave strips around the trees. Thanks!

(Chances are that next time he will do it with pride. It still may not be perfect, but who needs perfection?)

The biggest drawback to practicing this skill is "but. . . ."
"The bed looks nice and that corner is clean, *but*. . . ."
"The grass looks nice, *but*. . . ."
Usually the "but" negates the positive message. The last part is remembered—not the first.

It is almost certain that most of you are saying, "But how will they ever learn unless someone tells them what is wrong?" These examples should be distinguished from teaching-learning situations. Either the teenagers in the examples weren't interested enough to do the job right, or their concept of "good" was different from their parents'. People who are encouraged rather than criticized also learn a lot on their own. If your son, for instance, develops a real pride in cutting the grass, he will get even better at it than you—without anyone ever pointing out his mistakes.

Let's look at some other examples.

Example 3

Your son brings you his algebra homework to check. There are three right answers out of ten. You say, "You did this one well. You followed all the correct steps, and the answer is right. You also did well with questions 5 and 10." Your son may ask about the others and will probably be very eager for your help. But if you say, "They're almost all wrong; try again," you will have an angry, discouraged son who will probably not do the homework at all.

Example 4

"Martha, it's almost two hours since we have yelled at each other. I just wanted to thank you for your efforts. I will keep trying too."

Example 5

"It is so pleasant, Mary, when no one argues at the table. I appreciate your efforts to keep peace."

Now it is quite possible that Mary didn't make any effort at all; maybe nothing came up to fight about. That's all right. The positive statement will remind her and will encourage her to try.

Example 6

Kevin is supposed to clean the kitchen, but he always forgets or neglects some part of the job. Counters are left dirty, and sticky dishes are still in the sink. You say, "It was nice that you re-membered part of the counters tonight."

Example 7

"When I came home today, the stereo was at a very reasonable volume. I appreciate your cooperation."

Example 8

"I forget to mention this, but I really am pleased with the way you are always home at a reasonable time. I never have to worry about you."

Example 9

"How nice that you cleaned all this without my even asking. Thanks!"

Focusing on efforts and contributions is difficult, but it is amazing what a difference it can make in the home. Perhaps thinking of your own situation will help convince you of its importance.

Consider this possibility. You work hard all day and then come home and cook a special meal. You put it on the table proudly and sit down in anticipation of some response. The 16-year-old looks quizzical and asks, "What is this?" Not exactly what you are looking for, but he's a hamburger freak, so he can be excused. Your spouse takes a few bites and simply says, "These place mats are kind of dirty." Place mats? What nerve!

Now, honestly, what are the chances that you will put extra effort into making a meal tomorrow night, or even ten nights from now? The fun and pride are gone. Anger and resentment may well lead you to do the minimum for a while.

How would you feel if the 16-year-old had said, "You know, I usually hate fancy stuff, but this is really good," and perhaps if your spouse had said, "I can't believe how good you are at using just the right seasonings."

Imagine that you have just spent half a day washing windows and someone says, "There's a spot in this corner." How do you feel?

Think of another situation. The dog ran wild through the house and knocked over a lamp, the washing machine overflowed, and it looks as if you haven't cleaned for a week. The 17-year-old observes, "Dad, this place is a mess," and the 14-year-old smiles and says, "You know what I like about you? No matter what's happening, you always look as if you're handling it. Here, let me give you a hand." How do you feel now?

It's the same with teenagers. If we put them down and point out all their mistakes, they become angry and resentful and will be much less cooperative. If we mention at least one positive thing about them, it can make a big difference. It encourages them to try again; it encourages them to cooperate. It makes them feel better about themselves.

Here are a few examples to help you practice this critical skill. They are followed by sample responses.

Practice 1

Your 14-year-old son decided to surprise you by making supper. He overcooked some expensive meat, and the vegetables taste like mush. What do you say? What do you do?

_____

_____

Practice 2

Your daughter wanted to help with the laundry. The new jeans she washed with the white shirts created a problem. She is angry with herself and terribly embarrassed. What do you say? What do you do?

_____

_____

Practice 3

Your son used the car and decided to put gasoline in. Regular was cheapest, so he bought that, when unleaded is what the car takes. What do you say? What do you do?

_____

_____

Practice 4

Your daughter is proud of her ability to repair things. When the dryer failed to work properly, she was sure she could fix it. Now the dryer doesn't work at all, and you have to call the repair person. What do you say? What do you do?

_____

_____

Practice 5

Your son has learned how to check automobile fluids in a class at school. He wanted to surprise you by filling your radiator with water. What he didn't realize is that he should have added antifreeze instead. What do you say? What do you do?

_____

_____

Practice 6

It's 95°F in the shade, and you have no air conditioner. You come home and find a hot but proud daughter. She has just made a cake that had to bake for an hour in the oven. What do you say? What do you do?

_____

_____

The following are sample responses for the practice exercises. There are many more possibilities.

Practice 1

"You are so thoughtful to help me out by cooking dinner. Thank you!"

"Please don't apologize. Learning to cook takes time. What is really important is your thoughtfulness."

"It was such a relief to come home and find dinner ready."

Practice 2

"You wanted to help, and I really appreciate that. One way we can solve this is to soak the white shirts in bleach for a while. Would you like to try that? I've made this mistake plenty of times myself."

Practice 3

"We weren't very clear about which gasoline to use. The important thing is that you wanted to pay for your share of the gas. That was very considerate of you."

Practice 4

"Even good repairers like you make some mistakes. The important thing is that you were willing to try. You have saved us a repair bill in the past, and you will probably save us many more in the future."

Practice 5

"It's really good that you are learning so much about cars. What is even nicer is your thoughtfulness in trying to help. Actually, it's probably better that we flush the radiator out this year anyway."

Practice 6

"Will that taste good tonight! Maybe we could eat on the picnic table."

SUMMARY OF COMMUNICATION SKILLS

This chapter and Chapters 8 and 9 provide the information you need to make major changes in the way you and your teenager communicate and cooperate. If you follow the guidelines presented in these three chapters, you can make major, positive impacts on your family. But you can't just decide to do it one day and expect everything to be better immediately. The process is slow and difficult. Anyone who tries to change behaviors all at once becomes very discouraged and gives up within a short period of time, like the person who goes on a diet and gets discouraged if pounds aren't shed in a day or two. It's impossible to change many behaviors all at once. Proceed slowly. Build a solid foundation. Take it a step at a time.

Step 1

Begin by setting aside half an hour a day when you will avoid making negative statements. Don't try to make positive statements; just say nothing.

Mary comes home and drops some things at the door instead of putting them away.
    Say nothing.

Charlie begins fighting with Mary.
    Say nothing.

Now Charlie is teasing the dog.
    Say nothing.

Let's face it. Half an hour of that is about all you can stand in one day when you are just beginning. Try half an hour the following day. When it begins to be easier, try it for a little longer. Make it possible for yourself to succeed. Don't push too hard, too fast.

Step 2

As you begin to lengthen the time during which you avoid making negative statements, also begin to practice some of the skills discussed in this chapter and in Chapters 8 and 9. Perhaps the first week, you can try to say one encouraging thing a day. That's enough to start.

If everything goes well, the second week you can try to make one encouraging statement a day and to reflect feelings three times a week.

Step 3

Keep a chart of your successes. Don't dwell on "failures," for there are no failures in this project. *Anything* you can do to

	Sun.	Mon.	Tues.	Wed.	Thurs.	Fri.	Sat.
Avoided making negative statements							
Restated							
Reflected feelings							
Used "I" statements							
Accepted doer, if not the deed							
Focused on resources and strengths							
Focused on effort and contributions							

reduce negative statements and increase positive ones is an improvement. All you can have is success—even if in the beginning you can measure it only in minutes. Write each success down so that you can see how you are doing. This is a long, difficult project. You need a visual reminder of how well you are doing. Look at the sample chart, but feel free to develop your own. Charting your successes is not an idle suggestion; it will make a big difference in your perceptions and in your behavior.

Anyone who can become a consistently effective, positive person with teenagers in less than six months deserves every award available. Most parents will need longer than that, and many will find that new behavior is sporadic at best. One day will be great; the next day will be more like "normal." That's all right. No one fails at this. Whatever progress you make is great. Reward yourself for progress and *never, never* punish yourself. It's not good for your kids, and it's not good for you, either. The more positive you can be about your own success, the better you will feel about yourself. And when you feel good about yourself, it will be even easier to help your teenager like himself or herself.

Chapter 11

When to Be Tough and When to Talk

How do you know when to be firm and when to listen? When do you say "no" and really mean it, and when is cooperation better? When do you sit down and talk it out, and when do you say, "It's going to be this way, period"?

Anyone who reads this book is likely to ask these questions. In some circumstances I recommend that you get tough; in others I say that getting tough will only make things worse. Sometimes I try to convince you that listening is critical, and other times I suggest that you cut off all discussion. So what are you supposed to do? There are no absolute rules, but there are guidelines.

WHEN TO ANSWER "WHY?" QUESTIONS

Do Not Answer

1. When your teenager is yelling and angry.

   Son: All the other kids get to go home at eleven. Why do I have to be in at ten?

   Father: You're to be in at ten. Period!

> *Daughter:* Why can't I get my hair trimmed every two weeks? You're so unfair and stingy.
>
> *Mother:* You have your hair trimmed every six weeks.

2. When the "why" has been explained many times before.
3. When there is no real need for an explanation—when the answer is almost self-evident.

"Why can't we have liquor at my party?"

"Why can't I stay out all night?"

"Why can't I drive to Alaska?"

Do Answer

1. When you are having a nice discussion and your teenager has a real need to understand your reasons.

> *Son:* Dad, I know I have to be in by ten, but if you could explain why, it would help me out a lot.
>
> *Father:* I'm a little worried about the kooks in our neighborhood. I get really concerned about you when you are out later. I know you feel no danger, and it is quite possible that this is just my hang-up, but that's the way it is.

2. When no real reasons have ever been given for rules that your teenager feels are unreasonable.

"Because I say so."

"You're too young."

"I was never able to do it."

"Your father said so."

These are not *real* reasons. They are avoiding the issue or are put-downs. Real reasons come from real concerns. They are genuine. They may not always make sense, but they are honest.

> *Mother:* It may seem like a really unreasonable rule to you, and maybe it is. But I can't make my fears go away. I don't want to be unreasonable, but I don't want to feel like a bad parent either.

3. When your response could use an explanation.

Daughter: Why can't I go to Jumbo University?

Father: If I keep my current job, we probably could afford it, but quite frankly, the way my company is losing money, I can't be sure I will have this job much longer. Perhaps if you could start somewhere cheaper, I might be able to swing it when my situation is more secure.

WHEN TO LISTEN AND WHEN TO STOP A DISCUSSION

Stop a Discussion

1. When more talk will merely escalate a power struggle.

Son: I'm *going* to go.

Mother: No you're not!

Son: I don't care what you say. I'm going.

Mother: (silence)

2. When your teenager is trying to make you feel guilty.

Daughter: I'm the only kid in school who has to wash the dishes every night.

Mother: Life is tough.

Daughter: But, Ma. . . .

Mother: (silence)
You can wink, smile, and exit. You don't have to go far or be gone long. The bathroom is fine.

3. When the dog knocks over your best piece of crystal, the potatoes boil over, two kids are screaming in the backyard, and your daughter says sweetly, "Mom, why is life so much easier for adults than for kids?"

If you're superhuman, sit down and have a wonderful discussion. If you're normal, growl a little and shut up. Talk about it later.

Listen and Communicate

1. When more talk can end a power struggle.

   "Janet, we are just fighting like idiots. Let's sit down and see if we can straighten this out."

2. When your son or daughter feels overwhelmed by what is expected.

   Daughter: Ma, I know you have to work, but babysitting for Tommy every day after school and all weekend is making me crazy. I can't see my friends or do anything normal.

   Listen *carefully*. Something has to be worked out. Hire someone to babysit for Tommy or ask for help from friends, neighbors, or relatives. Have your daughter get a regular part-time job and contribute to the babysitting costs as a cooperative gesture to help you out. She may also forgo some clothes or other things so that you can pay a babysitter.

3. During a special time that you set aside for this purpose. Some parents find it very profitable to allot a few minutes a day or a week for each child. It is their special time to do something or just sit and talk. When you have prearranged a time for this, there is less tendency to put it off or not do it at all because you are angry. You spend this special time together whether you are fighting at the moment or not.

WHEN TO STAND FIRM AND
WHEN TO COOPERATE

Stand Firm

1. When you are enforcing limits. If you and your daughter agreed that her allowance must cover her entertainment and if the allowance is reasonable, her request for more money to go to a second movie in a week is beyond the set limit. She doesn't go. Her pleadings or anger do not need a response.

You set a limit with discussion. You enforce it without discussion.

---

2. When you feel manipulated.

   Daughter: I washed the car for you.
   Father: How nice; thank you very much.
   Daughter: Will you let me use the car *now*?
   Father: No, you can't use the car, but thanks for washing it.
   Daughter: Is that lousy! I do all that work, and you won't even let me use the car.

3. When your teenager is *always* asking for exceptions.
4. If your teenager is out of control or uses drugs frequently, communication and cooperation are almost impossible. You need to establish strict boundaries to provide safety for your child. I *do not* advise you to do this alone. It is just too much to handle without some type of professional help or a strong support system. Read Chapter 5 to be sure that your teenager fits this description. No one would want to categorize a teenager with ordinary problems as being "out of control."

Cooperate

1. When establishing limits. While you and your teenager are agreeing on reasonable limits, discussion, cooperation, and listening are all-important. If you set limits and establish boundaries in an atmosphere of peace and respect, you will have fewer problems.
2. If you often have a gnawing feeling that all your power is slipping away and that you are manipulated more than most parents. Try to take a look at the situation as objectively as possible and see where letting go even a little might help reduce your feeling of powerlessness. Sometimes it is difficult to tell what is reasonable control and what is driving your kids away.
3. When your teenager is asking for an exception that is reasonable and is asking for it in a reasonable way.

WHEN TO DEMAND COMPLIANCE AND WHEN TO IGNORE BEHAVIOR

Demand compliance whenever your adolescent's behavior is clearly thoughtless or irresponsible. Leaving the kitchen in a total mess, letting the stereo blare after everyone else is in bed, taking the car without replacing the gasoline used, and talking on the phone for two-hour stretches are all thoughtless behaviors that should not be allowed. Forgetting to put something away, not hanging up a coat, or occasionally leaving shoes for others to trip over may also be thoughtless behaviors, but demanding compliance on every little issue will only make your home a nagging hell. It is best to save your demand for compliance for bigger things. Use cooperation to deal with day-to-day aggravations.

The following are examples of irresponsible behavior that requires action:

- Your 13-year-old daughter has accepted an invitation to go out with a 28-year-old man.

- Your 14-year-old son has agreed to spend a week in the mountains with another 14-year-old, and there will be no adult supervision.

These are obviously big issues that don't come up every day. Normal, day-to-day irresponsible behavior is usually best ignored or discussed. Don't dilute your effectiveness by demanding everything. You will end up getting nothing.

Irritating but harmless attention-getting behavior is usually best *ignored*. Such things include:

- Leaving a bedroom dirty
- Tapping fingers on the table
- Kicking a sister
- Fighting with siblings

Power struggles between you and your teenager cannot really be ignored. You simply have to withdraw from the fight, and sometimes that makes it seem as if you are ignoring the behavior. School problems are the most common cause of power struggles. Doing poorly in school, failing to complete homework, and skipping classes—these behaviors are your child's responsibility. It is rarely productive to fight over them.

You should *demand compliance* whenever the behavior is dangerous and preventable. Stealing, using drugs, and driving recklessly are examples. Simply demanding compliance in such situations will rarely work, however. Professional help for yourself and perhaps your child will be necessary so that you can learn how to demand compliance *effectively* in your particular situation. No book can provide enough information for each individual case.

Inadequacy is another game teenagers play. You should not be hoodwinked into assuming responsibility that your teenager should assume. You should not ignore this kind of behavior. You must dump the responsibility back in your teenager's lap:

Daughter: The wheelbarrow is too heavy for me.
(Tough; push it anyway.)

Son: I don't know how to warm up soup.
               (Then I guess you don't eat soup.)

Son: I don't know how to iron shirts.
               (I'll teach you, and then you're on your own.)

Daughter: I don't want to go to work today. Will you call
               my boss and say I'm sick?
               (No!)

Son: Joe is mean to me. Will you call his mother and
               complain?
               (No!)

Daughter: My friend had this big problem, so I talked to
               her instead of going to math. Will you call in
               and say I was sick?
               (No. You can discuss it with someone at
               school.)

WHEN TO FORBID A BEHAVIOR AND WHEN TO DISCUSS IT

Forbid the Behavior	Discuss the Behavior
1. When you do have control over the behavior. For example, you can enforce a ban on obscene language in your presence, and you can forbid your daughter to allow her boyfriend to stay overnight.	1. When you have no control over the behavior. In such situations, discussion and cooperation may be your only hope of influencing your teenager. For example, you can't forbid your son to use obscene language when he is among friends. How could you enforce such a rule? You also can't forbid your daughter to have sex. You can, however, make rules about sleeping with her boyfriend in your home. This situation has to be handled partly by forbidding and partly by discussion, unless you are usually home to enforce the rule.

Forbid the Behavior	**Discuss the Behavior**
2. When the behavior is clearly inappropriate. For example, you can forbid your son to have a party for seventy-five people or to attend a college that would place you in serious debt.	2. When you disagree, but it's not a choice that is yours to make. For example, you can't choose your teenager's friends, and you can't decide whether your son or daughter will go to college.

A good rule of thumb is never to forbid something unless you will be able to enforce the rule.

Chapter 12

Punishment and Alternatives to Punishment

In _Children the Challenge,_ Rudolph Dreikurs makes a big distinction between punishment and consequences, and with good reason. Punishment is just that: "You goofed, and you are going to pay." The "payment" often doesn't make any particular sense. In addition, the punishment is almost guaranteed to increase future wrongdoing.

The problem is worse with adolescents because their need to rebel is greater, so the "value" of the punishment is more negative than it is with small children. The more you punish, the worse the situation gets.

Consequences are different. Consequences can be natural or logical. They differ from punishment in that they make more sense. They follow more logically from the action that brought them about. For instance, the consequences of wearing expensive high-heeled shoes in the snow are that (1) you get wet, cold feet (a natural consequence), and (2) you will probably ruin the shoes, and no others will be purchased until the time agreed upon (a logical consequence). Both make sense; that is, they follow from the chosen action. Cold feet and ruined shoes are certainly better than yelling, screaming, pleading, and threatening as a form of retribution. They also make more sense than punishment such as forcing your daughter to stay in the house for a week if she wears good shoes in the snow. Some tried-and-true, albeit not altogether successful, punishments that parents use are discussed below.

POPULAR PUNISHMENTS

Grounding

Grounding is by far the most used and abused deterrent to crime in the parent-versus-teenager conflict. It ranges anywhere from "You must be in before eight every night, except on nights when there is a football game, play practice, or a tiddledywinks playoff," to "You will be in this house every minute you are not in school for the next three months."

Occasionally some form of grounding in certain situations makes sense, but most of the time it creates more problems than it solves. Keeping your son or daughter away from friends and social activities for a short period of time will not hurt, but if this goes on too long, it can cause havoc. Friends and social activities are essential during adolescence. In fact, a lack of friends on a regular basis is sometimes reason for concern. Keeping teenagers away from friends and activities is almost worse than denying them food. It can (1) upset social networks radically, (2) force your son or daughter to rebel even more, and (3) in some cases, result in severe depression.

The fourth reason to avoid grounding is that it doesn't work. It is a futile exercise that merely widens the chasm between parents and adolescents. The fifth reason is that grounding can frequently begin looking terribly ridiculous. Minnie does something she's not supposed to do and gets grounded for two weeks. This makes her very mad, so she does something else wrong. Now she is grounded for three months. "Three months is forever as far as I'm concerned," Minnie reasons, "so I may as well go all out. Three months or three years—what's the difference?"

Does that mean you should never use grounding to maintain order? Not necessarily. But if it's used, it should follow from the transgression, and it should probably be agreed on earlier. The punishment should fit the "crime."

Charlie had a midnight curfew on weekends, and he came in late two weekends in a row. His parents talked to him and asked what he thought the problem was. He said there was no problem; he was going to be on time next weekend:

Father: But you said that the last two weeks, so I think consequences should follow if this happens again. What would be fair?

Charlie: Well, I suppose you could have me come in earlier, but that will make it even harder. How about this? If I'm late again, I can't go out at all the following Saturday.

Father: That sounds fair to me. If you are more than twenty minutes late this Saturday, you will not go out after supper the following Saturday. Right?

Charlie: Right. But don't worry, Dad. I won't be late again.

The consequence is logical, it fits the problem, and it has Charlie's cooperation. In fact, it was his suggestion.

Mary could never make it home for dinner. She got so involved with friends that she was always late. It was agreed that if she was late one more time, the consequence would be coming home right after school for two days. That makes a fair amount of sense. But grounding a teenager for skipping classes, lying, or not doing the dishes does not.

Suspending Use of the Car

Taking the car away is another popular form of punishment for older teenagers. Driving the family car is a big privilege, but it need not be used as a club. If your adolescent causes an accident, is given a ticket for reckless driving, or drives off to another state instead of the local ice-cream parlor, it is quite appropriate to restrict use of the car: "You goof with the car; you don't use the car." That follows logically. Restricting use of the car for not cleaning a bedroom does not follow logically.

Forbidding Phone Use

Forbidding use of the phone is also a common punishment. Using the phone for a longer time than agreed upon can result in a phone ban. However, forbidding phone use as a punishment for coming home late does not follow logically.

One exception is a restriction on phone use so that a teenager can have more time to study. Occasionally an adolescent can't get a friend off the phone without being rude. Blaming the parents for restricted phone use makes ending a conversation much easier. It provides a convenient excuse. Such a restriction should be temporary until your teenager can learn more appropriate ways of saying "goodbye." Help your adolescent assume responsibility for his or her own rules and limits.

Denying Extracurricular Activities

Pulling adolescents out of sports, music, dance, or drama programs in the school or community is almost always harmful. The chance that this will change undesirable behavior is very slim indeed. In fact, it is much more likely that the situation—whatever it is—will get worse.

The more a teenager enjoys the sport or other activity, the greater the harm, the greater the anger, and the greater the rebellion when it is taken away. This form of punishment doesn't even work as a means of giving a teenager more time to study. It will probably just make the school performance worse. Studying isn't just a matter of time. It's also a matter of motivation, organization, and concentration. Forcing a student to drop something that he or she loves for something that is barely liked or even hated is a poor strategy.

If there are problems at home or at school, involvement in activities can be very helpful in eventually solving them. Doing something at school that is enjoyable may even encourage a teenager to study and may provide an incentive for better all-around school performance.

Forcing a Teenager to Quit Work

Forcing an adolescent to quit a job when he or she doesn't want to can also create more problems than it solves. High school students should not be working so late or so long that they have no time for anything else. A reasonable schedule is essential, and although parents must discuss with their child the amount of work he or she can handle, limits are still necessary.

Once limits have been set, though, it makes no sense to use work as a club. Most teenagers mature a great deal as a result of job responsibilities. Some who are not successful in school or other areas suddenly find a place where they are useful and important. This should not be tampered with arbitrarily.

IF NOT PUNISHMENT, THEN WHAT?

Punishment is usually not effective with either young children or adolescents. The use of consequences should drop dramatically during adolescence. The older a child becomes, the less controls parents should exercise. Cooperation and communication should take the place of consequences. By the time an adolescent is 18, parental controls should be negligible. The 18-year-old should make his or her own decisions about school, work, time to be in, how much socializing to do, etc. If an 18-year-old stays out all night, won't get a job, or otherwise is running the house, that is a different situation and demands a different approach. (See the discussion of totally out-of-control teenagers in Chapter 5.)

The fact remains that sometimes you will heartily disapprove of your son's or daughter's actions. You do not have to tolerate obnoxious behavior from your teenager. If you agree that punishment is not a long-term solution, how *can* you effectively change disagreeable or inappropriate behavior?

The first place to start is with yourself; you must change your pattern of behavior. First, determine what your normal response is whenever your teenager engages in the undesired behavior. Analyze your past performance. Then decide on an alternative response. Following are a few examples of undesirable behaviors and ways to deal with them.

Talking Back

You and Wally are having a heated argument, which Wally concludes with, "You dirty bastard—I hate you!" What do you say? Think of your usual response. If you normally yell back with choice epithets of your own, take a deep breath and in a quiet but firm voice say, "You will *not* speak to me that way!" Then exit immediately in a slow, deliberate fashion. Anything else that Wally says—negative or positive—should be *ignored*.

Or you might simply stare at Wally for a moment and, without saying a word, leave the room. It is best if you do not make yourself available for further communication for some time. Stay away from Wally long enough for both of you to calm down.

Later, talk to Wally in a very quiet and serious manner. Make it short and to the point: "I will no longer tolerate these attacks. They will stop *now!* None of us is perfect, and I understand that you occasionally become very angry, but I will not tolerate these attacks. If you become angry with me, you can tell me so or yell if you absolutely have to, but I will not tolerate name-calling." If you have been engaging in the same activity you say you deplore, you might add, "I know that I've been angry enough to say things I don't mean just to hurt you. I don't intend to do this anymore." And *don't* do it anymore.

If it happens again, repeat the same message. If this problem has been going on for a while, it won't go away overnight. Anyhow, Wally wants to get you to respond in the *old way.* He is much more comfortable with that. Refuse to play the same game. Don't give in! That is the only way you can end it. If you are consistent, the behavior should be reduced significantly, and you may even find yourself in a new position of strength.

Let's look at the same problem and another typical response. Do you cry, look horrified, or not talk for a week when your adolescent attacks you verbally? Then you need a new approach. If the new response is uncomfortable, make believe you are acting in a play. Do anything to help yourself change your response. You might even find yourself enjoying your new role. If you usually whimper and cry, the next time yell back at full volume.

If your tendency in the past has been to react with horror, the next time laugh and walk out. If possible, stay away for a few hours. Don't say where you are going, be gone for dinner, and then return with a smile on your face. Sit your teenager down while you stand, and firmly and briefly say that the party is over. The "mouth" is finished. You will not tolerate that kind of attack in your home. When it happens again, continue your new behavior. Do not go back to your old ways of responding. Your response itself is not as important as the fact that it is a different response. The person who changes the script has the power.

Tardiness

Joe comes to dinner late without a good reason (such as school, work, practice, or another planned activity). In the past, you have always made sure that his dinner was warm and waiting, even though you have pointed out how his behavior inconvenienced the whole family. Stop responding this way. Let Joe know that the next time he is late, he will fix his own dinner with whatever is left over. When he is late again, let him fix his dinner and clean up after himself. Do it with a smile, but *do* it.

Refusal to Pick Up Clothes

Christopher doesn't put his dirty clothes where he is supposed to on time. You're so sick of reminding him that you end up collecting his clothes yourself. Refuse to play maid or butler. Tell Christopher that his clothes won't be washed until the next scheduled laundry time unless he washes them himself. If there is any ironing to do, he will have to do that too. If he ruins any clothes (to punish you for being so mean), do not replace them. Pretend not to notice they're ruined (even if it's killing you). Basically, it comes down to this: Isn't abolishing a behavior that is driving you nuts worth the cost of the ruined clothes? For the price of a dinner, you can give your ulcer a rest. Look at it this way, and the ruined shirt or pants won't seem so bad. And besides, Christopher is the one who has lost the clothes or who will look shabby if he wears them. He bears the responsibility for his actions.

Bribery: Alternative strategy to punishment that doesn't work

Rewards should be distinguished from bribery. *Bribery* is defined here as offering a positive reward for doing a certain thing when the two are totally unrelated:

"If you get all A's, I'll let you use the car."

"If you don't miss any classes this year, you can go to Bermuda for a vacation."

"If you stop drinking, I'll buy you a new coat."

"If you get different friends, I'll take you to the ball game."

Forget this tactic. Even if it works, it's not good. Just as consequences that make sense should follow transgressions, so too rewards that make sense should follow good, responsible behavior.

If your son or daughter gets all A's, that is a reward in itself, and having a celebration is fine. It's nice to celebrate an accomplishment. But that's a lot different from promising use of the car or anything else in advance.

Encouragement can be critical in helping your son or daughter get to class, but again, getting to class is rewarding in itself. A bribe is not good even if it works. What will happen if your son doesn't like his job later on? Long experience with bribery will make adjustment later much more difficult. Someone will not be there dangling a carrot forever. Internal motivation is essential to maturity. Bribes short-circuit that developmental process. The difference between bribery and encouragement is very important; encouraging behaviors were discussed in Chapter 10.

SUMMARY

- Do not use punishment or even logical consequences with adolescents unless it is absolutely necessary. Try anything else first: cooperation, communication, or encouragement. These approaches are recommended not merely because they are better for the teenager but because they *work* better than punishment or consequences. Teenagers who still need to be "sat on" are not ready to be on their own. Absence of punishment is not permissiveness at all. It's an attempt to get the kid to grow up. Now really—does it make sense for a parent to proceed as in the following example?

  A 17-year-old senior still has a curfew and is grounded for not cleaning his room, forgetting to take out the garbage, and just about anything else that comes up. A year later the 18-year-old college freshman can do as he pleases in his campus apartment. When is this person going to learn to take care of himself, since he didn't learn before going to college? If the parents kept him a child too long, he will be home at the end of the first semester.

- If you must do something, at least use *logical consequences.*

- If you must use logical consequences, make every effort to keep reducing their use until none is used at all by the time your teenager has reached the age of 18. Punishment and contrived consequences keep teenagers immature.

- Since punishment has not worked, try to modify your adolescent's behavior by changing your responses to repeated obnoxious behavior.

Index

Author's Note

If you have any unanswered questions on how to live with your teenager, I would be glad to attempt to answer them.

Please enclose a long, stamped, self-addressed envelope, and write to me at the following address:

Marlene Brusko
c/o Spring Cove Associates
814 Beacon Drive
Schaumburg, Illinois 60193